ALSO BY DAN GOLDBERG

Stand Back A Second…Just Don't Fall Off The Edge

Lighten Up and Lead

The Entrepreneur's Guide to Successful Leadership (co-authored with Don Martin)

PROGRAMS BY DAN GOLDBERG

The Six Steps To Solid Sales Success™

The Seven Elements Of Successful Leadership™

Soaring To Enlightenment

The Secret to Living a Contented Life

Dan Goldberg

AuthorHouse™
1663 Liberty Drive
Bloomington, IN 47403
www.authorhouse.com
Phone: 1-800-839-8640

©Library of Congress, ISBN, Etc

No part of this book may be reproduced, stored in a retrieval system, or transmitted by any means without the written permission of the author.

Published by AuthorHouse 07/24/2012

ISBN: 978-1-4772-2124-2 (sc)
ISBN: 978-1-4772-2123-5 (e)

Back cover author photograph by Arlene W. Leib

Any people depicted in stock imagery provided by Thinkstock are models, and such images are being used for illustrative purposes only.
Certain stock imagery © Thinkstock.

This book is printed on acid-free paper.

Because of the dynamic nature of the Internet, any web addresses or links contained in this book may have changed since publication and may no longer be valid. The views expressed in this work are solely those of the author and do not necessarily reflect the views of the publisher, and the publisher hereby disclaims any responsibility for them.

Acknowledgements

I dedicate this book to my son Reni, my brother Jack, my sister-in-law Jane, my daughter-in-law Sonia, my dear Donna Macon, and my wonderful friends; Ron Goldberg, Cindy Clair, David and Myrna Ginsberg, Howard and Denise Stredler, Bill and Donna Miller, Don and Sue Martin, and Bud and Diane Batcher.

To my son Marcus, my daughter Reyna, my father Ralph, my mother Frances, and my aunt Toby, who have all left this earth but are with me daily.

I love them all.

To the thousands of students I've taught over the years, and to those I continue to teach. You have all taught me as well.

And, to all of you who read this book.

May you learn, grow and prosper from its words and from everything that life has to offer.

"Everything is meaningless except for love."
Ralph Goldberg

"Relativity teaches us the connection between the different descriptions of one and the same reality."
Albert Einstein

"Laughing at ourselves is the tonic that keeps us sane."
Unknown

Preface

Throughout our lives we experience things that are so unusual it becomes difficult to believe that others could possibly understand them.

We tend to feel that if we speak about these events; our friends, relatives and acquaintances would make light of what we view as life altering episodes.

Consequently, a wealth of knowledge is never revealed and life lessons are lost.

Soaring To Enlightenment is about incredible situations and the affects they had on the lives of the individuals involved. And…how the lessons they learned can change your life as well.

Its characters take us to places few have gone and fewer discuss.

Contents

Introduction

Soaring to Enlightenment is the story of two men who, while not always in close physical proximity, have remained best of friends throughout their lives.

We are led through a journey of experiences, knowledge and enlightenment that may seem undeniably unique yet can be as common as we want to make them.

As Ed Elias and Chaz Samuel walk along the streets of Philadelphia, sit in its parks, and visit its eateries and attractions, we get a look into the exceptional lives of two individuals who have lived through a view of life that few of us ever see. The events of Ed Elias' life have caused him, and consequently Chaz, to understand the abilities we all have to live richer, fuller and more experiential existences. Their lessons enable everyone to reach places that seem unreachable, see things that seem un-seeable and do things that seem un-doable.

Follow Ed, Chaz, and their longtime friend Gail Carlow, as they bring us into an incredible world that exists for each of us. All we have to do is have the desire to pursue, find and enjoy it.

Leading Up to Now

It all led up to now, everything in my life, all the joys and sorrows, laughs and laments, tragedies and triumphs led up to me relaxing in this park on a clear spring afternoon, in the center of Philadelphia, waiting for Ed.

Here I sit, on this wooden bench, contemplating my life while sipping on an iced green tea, as the smell of flowers perfume the air and the sound of chirping birds and children giggling serenade me. My thoughts wander into my happy childhood as visions of my mom cooking on a cold winter's night, laughing at my father's jokes, enters my mind.

I see my grandparents and aunt sitting around the dining room table laughing along with her while my brother and I look at our baseball cards and chuckle at our dad's humor. We all lived together in a big house on the corner of two main streets in the Northwest Section of Philadelphia.

My dad was a wise and intellectual man who never graduated high school. He read constantly and loved to joke, talk politics and theorize about life and sometimes dance around the house. My friends would come over just to speak with him, get his views on world events and ask for his advice. He was a "repairologist" he would say…repairing luggage and handbags in his little shop in Center City Philadelphia.

I loved my neighborhood, so many friends and so much to do.

And I loved going to the playground where I watched the pro basketball players duel in pick-up games during the summer and I also watched my brother play some of the best third base, shortstop and second base I'd ever seen this side of Mike Schmidt, Larry Bowa and Manny Trillo. What an athlete he was and still is.

My mind started to drift further into my childhood when I caught a glimpse of Ed entering the park. He walked so straight and deliberate. You could see that he was a man of confidence and clarity just by his gait. His body has always been fit and he's been exercising ever since I can remember. As Ed started striding closer towards me I noticed that he was carrying a small book. He was wearing his signature black tee shirt, dungarees, and black rubber soled shoes. His slicked back black hair framed his slightly tanned face while his baldpate reflected a bit of the crystal clear sunshine that we had been graced with on this cloudless spring day.

The square city block sized park, with its benches, fountain and lush green grounds, was filled with business people relaxing and eating during their lunch breaks, young mothers, along with a few young fathers, playing with their children, sitting on blankets, or walking with strollers…entering the park at one end and leaving at the other. I watched some college students play Frisbee and looked at the older couples holding hands and talking as they either walked the park or sat and viewed the surroundings.

Musicians strummed guitars. Young people with tattoos of butterflies and hearts, angels and skulls, ships and abstract designs, highlighted bodies that sported pierced noses, lips, eyelids and navels, talked and laughed, sang and kissed.

The entire square seemed like it was a giant tapestry of teeming life in its most pleasant state.

As Ed passed the gazebo in the center of the grounds he stopped to speak with an old man, someone he seemed to know quite well. They laughed and shook hands. Ed saw that I noticed his arrival and he motioned to me that he'd be a few minutes as he sat next to his friend who was seated on a bench. I couldn't wait to speak with him. He had become a mentor to me, filled with insights that were uncommonly clear and inspiring. He was also an extremely funny man whose humor was well known and whose levity and wisdom drew people to him.

Ed and I have been friends since we were kids. He was one of my buddies who would come over to my house and speak with my dad in the early evenings, sometimes staying until his mom would call to tell him it was time to come home. He would, at times, come straight to my house after school so he could ask my brother to help him with his fielding and hitting during Little League baseball season. And, I can't remember how many times we played whiffle ball out in front of my house, how many balls we "roofed" as they sailed for home runs onto the tops of the homes across our narrow street and how often he'd stay for dinner.

Over the years our friendship has ebbed and flowed. Business interruptions, relocation, marriages and children, had all created different textures in our relationship. But through it all, even if we hadn't seen each other for years, we remained in touch and always considered ourselves best of friends.

In high school he was one of the most popular fellows in our class. He easily made friends with everyone, and while not the best student, he could certainly hold his own with the elite when he wanted to. His intellect far surpassed his grades. After he graduated he went to college for a while and then into the service. I went to work, first selling shoes, then in a record store and finally back to selling shoes, while going to college part-time.

When Ed returned from the army he was his usual fun self, just a bit wiser and worldlier. Shortly after his return we both went back to the same college full-time and that's when things became extremely interesting. I was fortunate to be a witness to part of Ed's extraordinary journey.

The Fall of '68

In the fall of 1968 Ed Elias and I were students at the Community College of Philadelphia (CCP). It was his second "tour of duty" at the relatively new institution. CCP had opened its doors for the first time in September of 1965 in a converted department store. The old Snellenberg's building was on 11th street in Center City Philadelphia, between Market and Chestnut streets, two of the three busiest shopping streets in the city.

The "lobby" of the old store had become CCP's main area of activity. The ceiling was high and there were elevators and escalators that took students to the classrooms on the upper floors. The grandeur of the area had been replaced with the starkness of beige utilitarianism, somewhere between a government building's décor and the basement closeout space of its former self.

Little did Ed and I realize how much that image would mean to us for the rest of our lives.

On one particular autumn morning we had taken the train into Center City together as we did every weekday, walked the two blocks to school and entered the lobby.

As usual, we ran into friends and classmates, exchanging pleasantries and short conversations. One of our friends was a woman named Ruth Lettinger. She had a slight build, with very long straight hair that she tied back into a braid. Ruth always had an expression of calm and contentment about her, the demeanor of peace and the movements of a ballerina.

Ed often spoke with Ruth, but on this particular day he reached new heights with her…literally.

While they were in deep discussion he realized that he was watching himself and Ruth as they spoke, not from where he was standing, but from the ceiling of the lobby!

There he was, looking down on the two of them. Both Ruth and he were having a totally cognizant conversation and yet at the same time he had somehow left his body, in essence, separated himself from himself while being able to view his physical being, as well as hers, from above.

Ed watched himself in his dungaree jacket and dark tee shirt, jeans and boots, hair parted in the middle, flowing past his shoulders. And there was Ruth, dark shirt, brown vest, jeans and brown shoes. They were talking and he was looking at them from above, like a movie that he was in.

It didn't scare him or alarm him. It was too interesting, too different. Then, all of a sudden, he was back in his body once again. Something had created a small disturbance, a bell or a buzzer had gone off and that was enough to redirect his energy and bring Ed back into his body.

Ed excused himself from Ruth, walked over to me and instantly began to relate the entire incident in extreme detail. He explained it so vividly that it has remained clear in my mind throughout the years.

He wondered, "What was that?" "What had just happened to me?" "How could I have just done what I did?"

The experience fascinated and intrigued both of us but certainly Ed more directly. He said that it obviously wasn't a normal occurrence, yet it seemed so natural to him. "What was it?" Ed wondered again aloud. We then both went on with our scheduled classes and activities. But we knew that something had changed him, a subtle yet all encompassing change that has been a part of him since that day.

As my thoughts of that occurrence continued to blossom, I felt a hand on my shoulder. "Yo Chaz…how are ya?" It was Ed. Ed always calls me Chaz, as do most of my friends from my childhood, while my newer friends call me Charlie, that's how I instantly know what category of friend has left me a message on my voicemail. The folks who call me Charles or Mr.

Samuel are usually trying to get me to donate money, sell me something, or are members of organizations that I'm involved in through business or as a volunteer. Chaz still sounds the most familiar. The yo? Well that's just a normal Philadelphia greeting.

The Hand of Wisdom

I stood up from the bench and we gave each other a hug that came from years of love and friendship, the type of embrace that conveys deep caring without uttering a word. "How are you Ed? Whatcha been up to?" I asked. Ed and I hadn't seen each other for over a year. He traveled quite a bit during that time, as I had, and like so many dear friends do…he counseled me by telephone during some tough times early in the previous year when I really needed him. But this was our first conversation and meeting since last winter.

"Chaz, you won't believe where I've been over the last year and what I've been doing. It's finally come together, and now I know what I'm supposed to do with my time on earth," Ed said with one of his patented smiles as he continued. "Geez…I don't know what took me so long!

"Life Ed…life is what takes us so long sometimes," I said philosophically, knowing full well what *It* meant.

"You're right Chaz, it is life, and in this case it's also the distractions within life and an electrical short in my Chrysler," he replied with his dry wit and a smirk. "And you know what Chaz? I now really know what I'm supposed to do with myself in this life," he emphasized with a serious tone as we both sat down on the bench.

"What *are* you supposed to do Ed?' I chimed in – knowing that Ed has done so many things and been admired for so long by his friends, colleagues and the community at large.

"I'm supposed to change the tires on bicycle training wheels for retired meringue dancing guava farmers in Lithuania!" he said with a straight face as the gulp of green tea that I had just taken spewed out of my mouth in a fine spray and deposited itself all over an unsuspecting Chihuahua whose owner was walking it much too close to the heretofore unknown danger zone.

I apologized profusely and began wiping the poor dog down with the napkins I was holding around the container of tea. The dog, seeking revenge, started urinating on my right shoe. Fortunately my back pocket contained a few extra napkins! The dog owner, Ed, and I began to laugh those uncontrollable laughs that go on for minutes, seem to stop, and then regain their momentum when one of the former laughers takes a glance at one of the other participants. It finally came to an end about five minutes later when my sides felt like they were going to split wide open (probably depositing my internal organs on some cocker spaniel or better yet, pit bull) and my face, along with those of Ed and Mr. Leash Holder had become so red and wet from the tears running down our cheeks, that I was sure some good Samaritan was going to run over to administer mouth-to-mouth resuscitation.

The Chihuahua and his master finally departed and as they strode away from us the dog turned its head and looked at me for one quick moment as if to say…bite me!

Ed broke the short silence by saying "Just kidding Chaz! It has nothing to do with going to Lithuania."

"Really!?" I replied in mock surprise.

"Latvia Chaz…I'm gonna do it in Latvia!"

After about 30 seconds of me banging my fist on the bench while emitting a cacophony of laughs accompanied by snorting sounds that could easily be confused with the mating call of a Wild Boar, I eventually regained my composure.

"Come with me Chaz, let's take a little walk." Ed stated

A Walk With Perception

Ed and I strolled through the park as a warm breeze ruffled my white cotton shirt and sent the aroma of the food a couple had sprawled out between them on the bench on which they were seated, joyously traveling up my nostrils. "Tuna hoagie!" Ed said with a wink. "Makes me want to stop for some food. But not just yet…unless you're starved, Chaz?" he went on. "Later Ed, we have plenty of time and I'm not overly hungry anyway." I assured my friend. "Good, let's just walk," Ed replied as we passed through the southeast corner of the park towards the tree-lined streets of stately federal era townhouses.

As we walked, I experienced an odor that I hadn't smelled in years.

I looked down and realized that I had stepped in a present, probably provided by my favorite Chihuahua. I continued walking and scraping the bottom of my left shoe on every patch of grass and every curb available as Ed shook his head and chuckled.

"You know Chaz, people are amazing. We have so much power within our minds, bodies and souls but so few of us take advantage of it," Ed stated, bringing me back to the point of our stroll. While we walked his fingers flipped the pages of his small soft covered book, more as an unconscious exercise than as a man searching for the right paragraph, while his arms moved in rhythm with his stride.

"Let me read you something," he said as he stopped and brought the book to a comfortable reading distance, opening it to a bookmarked page.

"Energy and persistence conquers all things."

"Do you know who said that Chaz?" "You!?" was my quizzical and humorous reply. "Very funny Charles…very funny. I mean originally!" Ed said, while holding back a laugh as he continued. "It was a man who walked these same streets…Benjamin Franklin. And I'm sure he was one of those people who took advantage of a lot more mind, body and soul energy than your average bear." "I'm sure," was my response.

"It's the first word of that quote that I want you to think about," Ed said as we started walking again and turned the corner to head east. "Energy Chaz, energy is everything…including us. Do you remember that incident with Ruth at Community College?" "How could I forget it Ed, it left a profound impact on me." "Well Chaz, you know that it changed my life and it's led me to discover things that have drastically altered my view of what it means to be alive, how we interact with each other, what success and leadership mean and ultimately what the secret of life really is."

"Wow Ed, I had no idea that you've taken that experience to such a level," I said, struck by the enormity of his statement.

"My friend, it's quite a journey but most definitely worth it," Ed related – his eyes looking intently at the sky while we paused for a moment.

"What's the final destination like Ed?" curious to know about the journey's end.

"Oh Chaz, there isn't a final destination, per say, it's the journey that's the destination. The whole trip is a revelation. It's so incredible yet so many people don't even notice it. Blows my mind Chaz…it really does. And… there's women, lots of 'em!"

"Huh? What did you say Ed?"

"Nah! Only jokin' but I knew I'd get your attention Mr. S," was Ed's response.

He was always great at keeping me on my toes.

"Remember this Chaz…life should be fun and there should also be lots of funny in life. I once read somewhere that, *'Laughing at ourselves is the tonic that keeps us sane.'* That's one of my favorite sayings…it really sums up an important aspect of life quite well. People spend so much of their lives thinking about the past while not focusing on the all-important present and their plans for the immediate, mid-range and distant future. There are so many neat things out there just waiting to be experienced! Plus, too many people take life way too seriously and harbor those energy zapping emotions; regret, guilt, jealousy and worry, not to mention greed and hate. And they actually think that material things, business success and position are more important than loving others and themselves, laughing and hugging and enjoying the fruits of nature. It's sad, very sad. And it's perpetuated by our society. It takes a strong person to see through it. That doesn't mean that you can't enjoy the finer things in life. What has happened however is that so many people have allowed those things to control them, instead of the other way around."

I thought about Ed's statement. How right he was. Earlier in the month I had a conversation with a real estate agent who told me that she had recently sold a large home to a couple. She had a feeling that they couldn't afford it but the wife was so intent on buying the house that they both decided to go ahead with the purchase. The agent went on to describe how they couldn't afford furniture or much else to outfit the new home. She ended the story by telling me, "You'd be amazed at how many people buy homes they can't afford! And the cars they drive up in…you'd think they were billionaires."

Yet they buy into the perception that what they show materially is who they are. They're so into impressing others that they create undo stress and anxiety for themselves and ultimately many of these marriages and families end up in divorce or disharmony.

The story reminded me of a something my father would always say, "The only thing that matters is love. Everything else is meaningless."

It also reminded me of two stories from back when I was a kid.

Childhood Lessons

During the summers I would spend some time at my dad's store. One week I went to work with my dad each day. Every morning around the same time I'd see an old black and white Chevrolet pass the store driven by an older gentleman. On my last day of that week, as the car passed by, I asked my dad if he knew who the man was who drove that old black and white Chevy. "Sure Chaz…that's Mr. Strawbridge," My dad replied. "Mr. Strawbridge!" I responded, knowing full well (even at that young age) that Mr. Strawbridge was one of the wealthiest men in Philadelphia and owner of the Strawbridge's department store chain. The flagship store and his office were diagonally across the street from my father's store. "Can't he afford a new car?" I asked in amazement.

My dad's remarks have resonated with me ever since. "He's Mr. Strawbridge Chaz…who does he have to impress? Most old money people drive Fords, Chevys and Chryslers. It's the new money people who try to impress each other. They're the ones who drive the fancy cars! In fact, if you think about it, if you're secure in who you are…what difference does it make what you drive?"

It's a lesson I'll never forget and is reinforced by my next anecdote.

This story is about my grandmother. She was an immigrant from Eastern Europe who spoke what we called "Fancy Broken English," or English with a heavy accent. One day she went shopping on South Street in Philadelphia. A street, known today for its eclectic shops and restaurants and for the famous song with that great opening line, "Where do all the hippies meet? South Street! South Street!" Much before the term hippies meant those of the long- haired variety.

In my grandmother's day South Street was filled with clothiers, furriers and bridal shops. My grandmother was a down-to-earth woman who was as comfortable in a housedress as she was in a gown, but her preference was a housedress. She had married my grandfather in the early 1900's. He had come to the United States from Eastern Europe as well and worked his way up from window washer to owning a large engineering company that would wind up building or refurbishing some of the most well-known monuments and industrial plants in the city. On this particular day she had decided to go shopping for a mink coat (long before there was any political correctness applied to such items).

As she walked into one of the furrier stores with her friend, who was also attired in a housedress, the saleswomen said something derogatory to another sales associate in my grandmother's native language – not realizing that these women in their housedresses understood exactly what they were discussing. It was obvious to my grandmother that both of the saleswomen thought that there was no way that she could afford a mink coat.

My grandmother and her friend proceeded to walk out of the establishment and walk next door to another furrier who treated them with respect and kindness. After completing the purchase of her new mink coat, my grandmother felt it appropriate to return to the original store attired in her new purchase and in her native language explain to the two saleswomen how wrong it was to judge people by their appearance! Needless to say, as my grandmother related, the two saleswomen were left dumbfounded with their mouths wide open as my grandmother and her friend exited the store.

I always loved those two stories and thought how well they related to Ed's comments

History in the Present

We had walked ten city blocks and were now passing colonial style homes built in the 1700's. All of them seemed to be immaculately groomed, their flower boxes overflowing with reds, yellows, purples, greens and just about every other color imaginable. I always love to walk in the historic area. Thoughts of Franklin and Jefferson, Washington and Adams and all the other men and women of that era constantly remind me of the continuum of life.

When I lived in Center City I would think about what it must have been like 400 years previous, before the Europeans arrived, before the buildings were erected and the roads and streets were put in place. I would sit by my window at night and image the forest, the Native American settlements, and the smells of nature where there now were the sounds of trucks and cars and the odors of restaurant food and bus fumes flowing through the air.

"These streets Chaz…they talk. They create visions in our minds. And if we listen deeply enough they tell us stories. Just like the houses do, and the graveyards, and the churches and synagogues. These 18th and 19th century buildings bring thoughts into our minds that are almost memories of a time during which neither of us were alive. Do you feel it?" Ed said.

He had transformed me back in time. Everything around me, including the "Belgian block" side streets and colonial lights, were conveying the energy of a budding nation. The cars and tourists, buses and residents, seemed almost out of place. I could feel it…the forces of long ago tugging at my mind.

"Yeah, I can feel it," I replied waiting to hear his response.

"Where do you think the energy that all the people and animals, buildings and infrastructure emitted from that era is?" Ed asked.

I had never contemplated that question, and to be asked it startled me. "What do you mean…isn't it gone?" I answered after a moment of pensiveness.

"Well if it's gone where is it? Where did it go? Is it all in Pittsburgh, Oklahoma City, Boise, or your cousin's house in Boca?" he countered.

"Energy flows, it doesn't really disappear. Some of the energy may be in different forms or places, but it's still with us, the same energy that Washington used to keep his men motivated at Valley Forge, the same energy that Franklin used to run his printing presses, the same energy that people used to build the underground railroad, to help free the slaves in the mid 1800s, under some of the structures we're passing right now. It doesn't go away, it just doesn't," Ed relayed with certainty.

"So what you're telling me is that everything that ever happened is still with us in some form or another."

"That's right Chaz and that energy enables us to transcend what we think are our everyday realities into something much greater. If, as the saying goes, people are breathing a molecule of Julius Caesar's last breath right now, how does that change your view of history, yesterday, now, tomorrow and your ability to emit, receive and understand the power of energy?"

"Ed," I said awed by the depth of his words and my visual concept of it, "where does someone start in order to build a comprehensive understanding of it?"

"Good question Chaz!"

"Start by thinking about your life. Don't focus on what I mentioned before… the useless emotions of regret, jealousy, worry and guilt. They zap your concentration and divert your energy. Think about your life and look at it from an energy perspective and tell me what you see Chaz."

"I see a man who enjoys laughing and has wonderful friends, a loving family and a measure of financial success, but I also see a man who has a lack of focus, someone who – all too many times – is in life and business situations that he doesn't enjoy, he goes along for the ride, taking the path of least resistance, doesn't use the energy that he has in the most effective way, and a man who's not achieving what he really, truly wants out of his short time here on earth…and that's just for starters pal."

"Very good Chaz, I think you're gettin' it now buddy! Serious introspection! It's tough to move to a new space until you understand the old one. Understanding yourself is the foundation of growth…the necessary base for moving ahead."

Focusing Your Energy

"Focusing your energy is like using a laser. It can take you to places you never thought you would reach. It's all about transcending your physical self," Ed stated as we rounded the corner.

I was still contemplating his last statement when I realized that we were now in front of Independence Hall, which I always found to be an inspiring place. Every time I walked or drove by it I was instantly transmitted back in time, much in a way that Ed had mentioned earlier. Being the history buff that I am, I would periodically take in the city's past by going on tours of the buildings, gardens, parks, and museums on the spar-of-the-moment. And Independence Hall and the Liberty Bell, which was now across Independence Mall, were two of my favorite stops.

We walked around to the back of the majestic building where the famous statue of Commodore Barry stands and the plaques explain how it was The State House of Pennsylvania and how our nation was born within its walls. The Declaration of Independence and the Constitution were both debated and signed in this red brick structure. I thought deeply in reference to what Ed said about energy and contemplated what the magnitude of the directed energy flow must have been like during those monumental days.

"Let's sit for a while," Ed directed as he walked us over to a bench with a view of the Hall and the Mall beyond and jokingly gestured towards my seat on the bench as if he were an usher in a theater.

It seemed like Ed was gushing with enthusiasm and bursting to fill me in on something. "I've kept much of this to myself over the years, but now I know it's time to tell you and others."

"I'm honored that you've chosen to tell me," I said sincerely

"Hey pal, if I can't tell you, and you're the first one I am telling, then who else can I tell?" Ed responded.

"Before you start Ed I do have a couple of questions for you, OK?"

"Sure little buddy," was Ed's reaction as he slipped into his Gilligan's Island Captain's imitation.

"What did Franklin and Jefferson use to wipe themselves with after they went to the privy? And how come nobody ever talks about that stuff? Plus did they wear cotton clothes in the summer, because it gets pretty darn hot in this town in the summer and every time I see a picture of those dudes and dudettes they're wearing hot looking (and I don't mean hot looking in the sexy sense), I mean hot looking in the throw a block of ice down my woolen shorts sense."

"Stop it!" Ed said as he doubled over in laughter, "I can't laugh anymore or my contact lenses'll pop right out of my eyes. But the thought of Jefferson calling out for another bushel of leaves is really funny. Franklin however, probably invented something to take care of the dilemma."

"Chaz, you're a trip and I must tell you that there's absolutely nothing better than laughing, nothing!!"

"Ahem…so may I continue Sir Charles?"

"But of course," was my reply

"After my experience with Ruth at Community College I knew that something special had happened to me. But you know me…I had to do research on my experience to find out if there was any additional information on the subject.

"Chaz, I am by no means a physicist. In fact, you may remember that in high school I had to beg Mr. Brooks in order to pass his physics class." "And buy him that Chevy Malibu too," I interjected. "Stop it I said!" Ed yelled. "Besides, it was a Pontiac Grand Prix. And may I continue?" "Of course Ed…but you know how much I enjoy our bantering back and forth and our puns." "Yeah, I know…isn't that why Mr. Finkelstein in English used to call you Rapunzel?" "Indeed," was my response with glee that Ed remembered that bit of high school trivia.

"Back to my point pal, what you may not know is that I've always been fascinated with the subject. After all, physics is about energy and energy is about everything."

In high school Ed kept everyone entertained with his impressions, jokes and all-around good humor, but sometimes it interfered with his academic excellence. That's why he had to beg Mr. Brooks to pass him in physics class. And there really weren't any cars involved.

As he continued to speak I could see his intensity grow.

"Dr Samuel," he said jokingly and then changing his tone to emphasize the seriousness of what he was about to tell me, "I intrinsically knew that there was a physical explanation for what had transpired in that encounter with Ruth. Everything that happens on our planet has an explanation based on physics and energy. The only question was whether or not it had been *discovered.*

"I began to do research in libraries, checking through books and periodicals, from Princeton scientific journals to The Meaning of Relativity by Albert Einstein, from Rosicrucian works to the Edgar Cayce readings. I would ask people, you may recall, in a very cautious manner, for fear that they might think that a few screws in my head needed to be bolted a little tighter, if they knew of situations like those that I had experienced. Some actually said, 'Yes!' Whew, what a relief, I would think." Ed's own energy was flowing quite readily now as he continued his informative monologue.

"After straining through untold amounts of information I began to understand that there was a term that closely, but not exactly, approximated what had happened to me. It was called astral projection. And even though astral projection seemed to happen at night, to people who would leave their bodies in almost dreamlike situations, it was as close to my occurrence as I could find."

No Silver Chord

I had certainly heard of astral projections, read a number of articles on the subject and watched a slew of television documentaries about it…but somehow had never put Ed's experience and astral projection together. Perhaps I had just forgotten about Ed's and Ruth's encounter during that period of my life.

Ed continued, "However, one element eluded me – the silver cord. Everything I read about astral projection mentioned a silver cord that connected the physical person, usually at the navel, to the spiritual person as they traveled. But there was no cord in my situation, just free movement with nothing connecting the spiritual me to the physical me except the inherent energy.

"Then I thought about some instances when I was a kid living back in the old neighborhood.

"Do you remember that big stone house on the corner of Upsal Street and Stenton Avenue with the blue railings around it, that I lived in years and years ago?" Ed asked.

"Sure, that's the one where both the S *and* L buses used to stop in front of…right?" I asked rhetorically.

"Exactly," Ed confirmed. "Well back when I was a little guy I remember laying in bed one night. My bedroom was on the second floor of that three-story house. I shared it with my brother Jacob.

"My room was dark; the lamp on my night table had been turned off just a few minutes earlier by my mom, as she and my dad said good night to me and my brother. The ceramic horse base and goldenrod lampshade were still visible because my door was open and the light from the hallway reflected off that palomino lamp I loved so much. My eyes followed the light illuminating the hall as it blended with the glow emanating from lights that lit up the main entrance of the house below. I looked longingly through the open door, wishing that I was downstairs having fun, laughing and playing, especially since I knew my parents were having a get-together.

"As the evening passed I could hear my relatives and other friends of the family arriving downstairs. The doorbell would ring, the screen door would open and another person, couple or group of people would enter. They were gathering to attend another "cousins' club" party. How I wished that I could get out of bed, walk down the winding staircase and be a part of the festivities.

"More and more people kept ringing the doorbell and coming into the house. I could hear them. I recognized their voices, including your mom's and dad's, Chaz. I wanted so much to be a part of the fun. But I knew that my mom and dad had told me that it was my bedtime and that there was no way to change that.

"Then, suddenly, there I was, downstairs watching everyone enjoying themselves, telling jokes, talking, drinking and eating, shaking hands and holding hands, laughing and relaxing. However, I wasn't exactly there. I was floating above them all, maybe three feet that's all, and I had the ability to witness the entire scene. I soon realized no one could see me. Yet, I could see myself. I could look down and see my body, arms and legs as I floated along. I was like an invisible bird. I loved it. I was king of my little world, the great observer. And no one, not even my mom or dad, could see me. It was amazing.

"The night went on and so did my invisible journey. I watched as people came and went, looked at the food as it kept getting replenished, smelled the aroma of cake and roast beef, coffee and chicken and heard the sounds of men and women telling stories and exchanging pleasantries.

"And when it was over I didn't tell anyone. Not my brother or my friends, not anyone! When I got up the next morning I did the usual things we did back then. I went to school and studied arithmetic and social studies, painted during art time and talked about baseball while I played in the schoolyard at recess. When I came home, I bought my ice cream and played catch with my friends…I'm quite sure that you were there pal. Later, I did my homework, ate my dinner, talked to my mom, dad, brother, and grandparents and aunt, who also lived with me, and went to bed.

"A month later it happened again. My parents had another party and I was able to do my flight above the people once more, and the next time and the next until it became just another thing that I could do. And never a silver cord.

"But I still didn't tell anyone.

"Now I realize that I had been given an incredible talent back then, the ability to know that I could separate my self from myself. I could see other people and myself. I could stand back and observe while being out of my body. What a gift that was!

"As I grew older and put my energies in other directions, that wonderful gift faded from my thought process and memory.

"Yet it wasn't until the last year or so that I was able to put two and two together, my childhood experiences and my experience with Ruth and all the subsequent ones that it has all become so clear!

"Chaz, at 6 years old I was able to travel to an extraordinary place, a place where the world was opened to new vistas and wonderful broad views and years later I was given that gift again and again.

"But most importantly, I also recall knowing deep inside, that I wasn't the only one who could do this. And I'm convinced now more than ever that everyone on this planet has the same ability. It's about energy…all about energy."

I sat there mesmerized by Ed's revelation, which was quickly becoming mine. I had no idea about Ed's childhood experiences or the fact that there were other events after the situation with Ruth. Plus, his statement about everyone having the capability to leave his or her physical self fascinated me. I wanted, and needed, to know more.

Of Radio, Television and Energy

Ed raised his book up again and opened it to another page. "Tell me what you think of this quote," Ed said as he paused to glance at my face for a positive response, which I quickly gave him. He then turned back to the page and read.

"There's a ripple effect in all that we do. What you do touches me, what I do touches you."

"Wow Ed, that's a pretty profound statement. It sums up the interrelationship of everyone and everything on the planet. It really puts the effect of the energy we send out into perspective," I replied still deep in thought.

"Precisely, and you added something there that I'd like to discuss. You said...the energy we send out. Whoever authored those words knew what he, or she, was talking about. Everything that happens on this earth affects everything else!" Ed said emphatically.

"Let's get into your statement about sending out energy, ok?"

I nodded my approval...and added, "Sure."

"You listen to the radio and watch TV, right?"

"Well hello Ed! Are you livin' on Mars or something? Did you have an intravenous triple espresso which sent the caffeine directly through your bloodstream and into your brain? Of course I do!"

"It was a rhetorical question Chazzy."

"Those radio and television signals are set to wave frequencies. So when you tune to channel 6 or 90.9 FM or 1060 AM, you're tuning your receiver to pick up a certain frequency…a certain wavelength. Your receiver processes those frequencies and voila, you hear, and or hear and see, the information you desire. Those waves are energy waves that move at a certain modulation, which differentiates them from other energy waves that move at another modulation. They can be low farther apart waves like those in a calmer ocean or higher closer together waves like those in a choppy or stormy ocean. Each different type of wave sends a different message and when you combine waves you get texture and more complicated messages. It's a simplistic way of describing it but you get it don't ya?"

"Sure I get it and I've always known it but rarely do I think of it. And I like your ocean analogy," I said as I visualized the Atlantic churning its waves against a sea wall.

"Thanks. So if your radio can pick up signals or energy waves and your television can pick up energy waves and the radio and TV towers can send out those waves, what do you think your mind does or can do?"

"I guess our minds do the same. We send out mental signals and receive them," I surmised.

"Sir Chazworth…you win the golden pretzel, Philadelphia's highest award for deductive reasoning! That's exactly what our minds do! I'd do a dance right now but I have a newspaper to read," Ed said with a wink. When he was younger that was his favorite line when someone asked him to do something he didn't want to do or go somewhere he didn't want to go. "Sorry I have a newspaper to read," he'd say and everyone would know not to press the issue.

"So using that premise, we already know that our minds can receive energy waves but it also means that our minds can be used as broadcast mechanisms and that our thoughts can be transmitted just like any other signal, right?"

"Whoa, hmmm…I guess you're right," I said after a pensive moment.

Ed was really getting me to re-think my whole understanding of the use of energy. I'd always thought of it as the stuff that came through wires and/or pipes into my home or was used in transportation or was harnessed using solar panels, but I never thought of it coming out of my mind in the way he described it. I know that we give off heat and use energy when we walk, run and participate in sports, but this was a somewhat different view.

"Keep goin', you're on a roll," I said realizing that I had set Ed up for another straight line.

"I am?" He said gently lifting himself off of the bench. "I hope it's not a Kaiser Roll with egg salad…it stains!"

"I knew it, I knew it…boy did I lay that one in your lap," I said with a groan. "And don't do a lap joke!"

"All right, I won't. But I want to get back to discussing being able to transmit and receive energy through our minds, ok?" Ed asked knowing my response as I shook my head in the affirmative.

Victor and the Light

"Do you remember Victor Carr from Mount Airy?

"Yep," I said recalling our friend from our old neighborhood in Northwest Philadelphia known as Mount Airy. Victor always wore a Second World War era Eisenhower style army jacket and his hair was usually worn in shoulder length tight curls. He was a slim young man who seemed to have a glow about him. One other thing I remember about Victor, he was almost always smiling, just a real nice guy.

"Well Victor and I had quite an experience related to thought and energy transmission.

"We were at Alan Coleman's second floor apartment in one of those big houses on Spruce Street in West Philly by the Penn Campus."

"I always liked Alan, he was extremely bright and a great person to talk to about philosophy and politics," I added.

"I don't know where you were that night, but I don't recall you being there…anyway, I remember wanting to speak with Victor who was somewhere else in the apartment. I kept thinking, Victor where are you, I'd really like to talk to you. The thought was intense and it repeated itself over and over again. Finally Victor appeared and as he approached me he said, 'I heard you calling, I'm sorry it took so long,' I was amazed. I hadn't physically called him, yet I was sure that he heard my thoughts. At the same time I took his comments in stride as if it was a natural occurrence.

"I was sitting on Alan's couch in the living room facing the kitchen straight in front of me, the hallway to his bedroom and bathroom was next to the kitchen and a bit off to the right. The couch was against the front wall of the apartment with the windows behind it. I can still recall the kitchen vividly. It was dimly light by a fixture over a dinette style table, the kind with a Formica top and chrome trim and sides. The yellow glow of what seemed like a sixty-watt incandescent bulb cast a shadow over the cabinets, appliances, table and chairs. The off white walls seemed to have an almost faint greenish yellow tinge. Victor proceeded to pull up a wooden chair and sit directly across from me.

"As we looked at each other to begin our conversation, a strange thing happened. All of a sudden a bright white beam of light with a slight blue tint appeared, emanating from the middle of my forehead to the middle of Victor's. It was in the same location that the mystics refer to as the third eye. There was no need to talk because all the information that Victor and I wanted to exchange was flowing into our minds along that beam of light. It was absolutely incredible. No sound, no voice, just pure thought.

"All during that time Alan's apartment had ceased to exist. We were no longer in an apartment; instead we were floating in the heavens. The kitchen, hallway, and living room had been completely replaced by the darkness of a clear night highlighted by the beauty of twinkling stars.

"While I'm recounting this to you it's as if I'm transmitted back to the apartment. That's how clear it is in my memory. As Victor's and my extrasensory conversation was ending, what I'll describe as frames of film appeared between us. It was like, when you watch an old sixteen-millimeter home movie and at the end the last few frames flash on the screen. The movie itself has ended and the frames look white with some colors quickly passing through them in the few split seconds that they can be viewed on screen, and then they're gone and all that's left is the light of the projector on the white screen. Those movie frames sliced right through our beam of light and ended our mental discussion.

"I was astonished," Ed continued. "I sat there for a second and then asked Victor. 'Did you see what just happened?' 'Yes I did,' was Victor's response with an astonished look on his face as well. So I asked him if he would recount what he saw, felt and processed. Victor repeated back to me exactly what I had seen and experienced. It was absolutely incredible."

"Ed you are really freakin' me out. Are you serious about all this or were you chewing on something that shouldn't have been growin' in your garden?"

"Come on Chaz! You of all people know that I wasn't heavily into that stuff. I was far too political during that time. In fact, to this day I can say that I missed out on most of substances that were circulating back then. My experiences happened when my mind was clear and things were not distorted or created through anything that could be smoked or ingested. That's why I know that everyone has this ability within them!"

"Wait, does that include bananas…you smoked bananas right?" I countered, remembering the time I actually put banana peals in the oven with my friend Glen and after they were sufficiently cooked, cut them up and smoked them. The only reactions we got were sore throats.

"Yea right, Mr. Mellow Yellow…me and Donovan," Ed said with a smile as he went on.

"That experience with Victor added new insights into my understanding of the capacity of the human mind. I thought about my encounter with Ruth and our, and I say our instead of my because I feel we all have this within us, ability to separate our selves from ourselves and view ourselves as if we're in a movie that we're watching. I realized that if we also have the capability to communicate through thought alone, as I could with Victor, then where could these abilities lead us as a species and as living beings?

"By the way I want to clarify one item in my last statement," Ed blurted out as if to make a specific point. "I say us as living beings because if humans can do it, I believe other species have these abilities as well."

And Other Animals Too

"It amuses me when I read certain self-help authors who state, rather unequivocally, that humans have higher intelligence than animals and possess attributes like free will and other skills that separate us from other species. I always want to call them up and ask them, 'How the heck do you know that?' It amazes me that some people can be so ethnocentric, or species centric, that they believe that other species can't possibly posses the same, different, greater, or more intuitive, faculties than we do as a species.

"If that were true, dogs and cats wouldn't be able to sense earthquakes and storms before they happen, or sense health problems with their masters that have been documented over and over again. How does anyone know that an animal doesn't have free will? After all, if humans were so great at the free will thing why do so many of us 'willingly' follow leaders who send us to our own demise when a bit of free will would certainly have prevented disaster. So I guess free will is a relative term. It reminds me of a quote from one of my heroes, Albert Einstein, *'Relativity teaches us the connection between the different descriptions of one and the same reality.'* Hmm...maybe in some cases it's possible that animals might even be more intelligent, and have greater free will then humans, n'est-ce pas? " Ed stated, adding a bit of French for emphasis. He always loved to throw in words from different languages out of the blue. I guess he could have said "don't you think?" or "no?" but the n'est-ce pas added just the right spice.

The mention of animals made me think about my old dog Poe. Poe had an uncanny ability of always seeming to know when I wasn't feeling up to par. She would give me more than her usual attention, cuddle up just a bit closer and make me feel loved. I would always wonder how she knew. Ed's point rang true – it must have been the energy that I was sending out. Poe could feel my pain and needs without me saying a word. I was communicating with her unconsciously. It makes sense, now that I think about it. The natural progression would be that if I could mentally communicate with my dog, then I must certainly have the capacity to communicate in the same manner with other people.

Then again, what was I communicating to Bear my cockerpoo who would jump up on me every time I walked in the house and on more than one occasion rip my suit pants in his excitement at my arrival. Hmmm… maybe I should have started sending out different signals before I put the key in the door!

Ed was really getting into it now. I had no idea about some of the things he told me. I had always thought that he filled me in on everything.

"Ed," I said curiously. "How come you never told me the Victor story before and I'll assume some of the other things that you're gonna let me in on?"

"I guess I felt that I wanted to fully understand what I was going through before I mentioned anything about it to anyone," was Ed's response.

I couldn't argue with that. While Ed and I shared just about everything, I think that there are certain situations that all of us seem to keep to ourselves.

As we continued our conversation it was becoming clearer and clearer how energy, in all its forms, was the propelling force in our lives. I was beginning to visualize Ed as something more than a friend and a mentor. He was the keeper of secrets that I couldn't wait to hear.

Something From Nothing?

Referring back to a statement that Ed made earlier, I asked him where he thought the energy was that he and Victor had used in such a focused manner. "Everywhere," he said. "It hasn't left us, that's for sure. It's still out there in the same way that we used existing energy to have that experience. See, when someone says that they're generating energy, the fact is that they're actually focusing existing energy for a different purpose. Everything's already with us, it's just a transformation."

Once again, Ed had revealed something that I hadn't really thought about. How can you create something from nothing? Something has to be there to begin with.

That led me to think about what it takes to become a success in life and business, be viewed as a leader by yourself and others, and create more happiness, contentment and prosperity for yourself and others. All the energy that's needed to accomplish those goals is already here. As Ed said, it just needs to be transformed and focused.

I was starting to feel more energized then I had in a long time, knowing that all the tools I needed to build a strong foundation for greater success in life and business were already in my tool belt.

"Tell me more," I pleaded with Ed. "You've got me hooked."

"Well, let's see. Let me preface the next story by expanding on a point I made earlier about the energy of people in history. To be more specific, it's the energy of everything in the universe. The Big Bang is still bangin'...that energy's still with us. So – when I speak about the energy of Washington, Jefferson, Franklin, and Julius Caesar, I hope you understand that they're only examples, albeit real examples. And, that I'm also talking about the energy of our solar system and the entire universe. It's always all around us.

Sure, gravity focuses certain amounts of that energy here on earth, but when you think about having the energy of the universe available to you it really becomes quite astounding."

"Ed, I think astounding is an understatement, if that's possible."

Bobble Heads

"No, I think you're right," Ed said as he turned to look at a group of tourists who seemed to appear out of nowhere. They stopped approximately ten feet from where we were seated.

There must have been twenty people in the group, many with cameras around their necks. Every one of them stood at attention as the tour guide, dressed in colonial garb, spoke about the men who came to this site over two and a quarter centuries ago to start America. All heads turned upwards as the guide discussed the steeple on Independence Hall and then their heads turned right as their attention was focused on another part of the building. And so it went, heads bobbing from one area to the next, while their bodies hardly moved.

It almost looked like a scene from "Saturday Night Live." The tour guide was really into a rhythm. Her mouth was moving at break-neck speed while her hands moved like conductors' batons.

Ed looked at me with an *"I can't believe what I'm seeing"* expression. All I could do was raise my eyebrows in amazement. I expected to hear "Stars and Stripes Forever" blast through a hidden loudspeaker as I began to hum the words to myself. They somehow fit the movement of the heads as they bobbled from one view of the Hall to another in perfect synchronization. Finally, I noticed fatigue beginning to set in as a woman wearing a "Wish I Was Here" tee shirt started rubbing her neck and the neck of her young son who was wearing an equally enticing shirt with the question, "Where

Am I?" emblazoned on the front. All I could think of was, "Like mother like son."

At last the Martha Washington look-alike guide was ready to move the group along. Not realizing that she had single-handedly increased the volume of purchases of pain relief rub and aspirin significantly in the City of Brotherly Love, she mistakenly instructed the group to "Quick, turn around, there's Ben Franklin!" "Ouch" was the first thing that came to my mind as an older man who had a baseball cap on that read "John Dear" in the colors of the *real* tractor maker's cap, but in substantially different type face, turned to see a man who portrays the great statesman and inventor, only to lose his balance. A young woman who was the spitting image of Colin Powell grabbed the falling gent on one side while another woman, who reminded me of cross between Carole Burnett and Connie Chung, pulled Mr. Dear back from his immanent demise.

The crowd gasped, as the once almost horizontal human regained his balance and took deep breaths as he expressed his appreciation to the two women. As the group checked to make sure all was ok with the fellow, I heard his wife say, "John, dear are you alright?" Ah ha, I thought...hunch confirmed. "Yes my dear," was his reply. All was now fine at the Cradle of Liberty as the crowd dutifully followed "Martha" toward the front of the building. As they were almost out of sight I heard young Mr. "Where Am I?" say, "Mom, where's Philadelphia?" along with his mom's response of "Right her Georgie...right here."

With the real life one act play over, Ed and I decided that it was time to eat.

Time for a Snack

Since neither of us had lunch and it wasn't yet dinnertime, Ed and I debated as to where to munch. Finally, we figured we'd take a walk over to one of our favorite places for a late-mid afternoon snack. Essence – the natural food store and café has been located a few blocks south of South Street for years. It had previously resided on the "hippest street in town" prior to its expansion.

Before deciding on Essence we went back and fourth between a Philly cheese steak from Joe's on South Street or something of a "healthier" variety. "Healthy" won, more for the lightness of the fare than for anything else.

As we released ourselves from the bench I felt a strange phenomenon. It was as if a cold breeze had stopped in front of me for a few moments. Even though the weather was clear and warm the air facing me was reminiscent of the sensation one gets when standing in front of an air conditioner. Walking away I sensed that the cold air followed me for a few steps before dissipating.

I stopped in mid stride to alert Ed.

"Ed, the most bizarre thing just happened to me. When I got up from the bench cold air seemed to be staring me in the face, in fact, blowing at my entire body as if I was standing in front of an air conditioner. It followed me for a few steps and then was gone."

"That was more than just cold air Chaz that was concentrated energy.

Perhaps it was spiritual in nature, maybe something returned to check out what we were up to?"

"Are you serious?" was my immediate response. Things like that are not normal occurrences in my life. I needed to know more about what Ed was discussing and what else had happened to him.

"I'm very serious. Energy's an awesome thing. It can move earth, bring us light, grow our food, enable us to walk and talk...why shouldn't it visit us in other forms? It goes back to what you said about '*astonishing being an understatement.*' For some reason I couldn't argue with that.

"Have you ever been overcome by a feeling like hurt, love, hope, or anxiety?" Ed asked – knowing full well that, like every other human, I have certainly experienced those states.

"Well focused energy has a hand in that.

"Back in the mid-seventies a good friend of mine in Los Angeles who was, at the time, a newscaster and radio personality told me about a man who was watching TV in his home on a mountaintop somewhere in Oregon.

All of a sudden the guy's television starts broadcasting shows and commercials from the '50s. And, by the way...this is long before cable, so it wasn't some nostalgia channel. What seems to have happened was that the original broadcast signal's focused energy had gone out into the solar system, possibly gotten caught in some gravitational pull or perhaps some other force, and turned itself back to earth and voila, this guys watchin' an original broadcast of I Love Lucy or some other show!

"And, Chaz...it's quite possible and makes perfect sense, doesn't it?"

The Joy of Seeing Gail

"Yes it does," I replied as Ed's words radiated once more. This day has brought new insights for me and I also think it has allowed Ed to discuss topics that he's wanted to speak about with me for years. We had left the grounds of Independence Hall and were crossing its southernmost boundary, Walnut Street, on our way further south to Essence. I was back at the thought of the cold air being something spiritual in nature, perhaps a being from the past, when we saw an old friend walking towards us.

Gail Carlow was part of the group that Ed and I hung out with at Community College and in Mt. Airy. She was a fun person to be around and loved to laugh and tell jokes. She had also been best of friends with Ed's old girlfriend Barbara. I always enjoyed being with her. Quite often she would coordinate the group's evenings, outings and parties. We all looked to her to keep us on track, since she seemed to know where everyone in the group was at any given time.

I hadn't seen Gail in a couple of years. She worked for the School District of Philadelphia the last time I saw her and had been in their employ for years. As she approached I noticed a big smile on her face, her shoulder length brown wavy hair bounced as she walked and her large brown handbag swung back and forth as she strode towards us. She was wearing dungarees, sneakers and a beige blouse. Seeing Gail zapped me back to thinking about when Ed and I would stop by her house to pick her up before we headed out for a night of fun.

Ed's joy was evident upon seeing Gail. He had a grin from ear to ear and he proceeded to skip a bit as we quickened our pace towards our good friend from days past. Of course we always felt, once a good friend, always a good friend.

Gail greeted both of us with big hugs and kisses. "Gee I love this woman! She was like a sister to me," I thought. Being with Gail and Ed gave me the feeling that everything was right with the world. The good, warm feeling of friendship squared.

"Whatcha been up to?" I asked Gail…wanting to hear about her life since the last time we saw each other.

"Well…I'm off today. I'm still at the School District. I took a personal day to get some things done that I haven't had time to do. I'm going on a trip to Iceland."

Gail traveled more than anyone I knew, except folks who were always hopping on a plane for business. I remembered when we were younger that she had gone to Iceland on her way to a backpacking trip through Europe.

"Goin' back to Iceland ay Gail?" I said with an understanding that she might not realize that I recalled her first sojourn.

"Wow Chaz, how the heck did know remember that I had gone there before? It was so many years ago that *I* almost forgot!"

"How could I forget your trip Gail and those incredible pictures? Hey, it may have been many moons ago, but the old noggin' is still working"

"Many, many moons ago and I can't believe you remember the pictures."

"Gail, that's not all there is to remember," Ed said.

"Chaz and I were just talking about the old days and I was recalling some of the things that went on with reference to energy. I certainly remember your involvement. In fact, I was just getting ready to relate an incident to him that you contributed to. It's really wild that you should show up now after all this time. Boy, it's great to see you!"

"Ed, I'll never, ever forget that time in our lives. It may have faded a bit but it's still so much a part of me," Gail responded with a sense of kindness, reverence and understanding in her voice.

"Sometimes I wish that we were all back there, going to school and hangin' out, but those days are over," she continued with a hint of melancholy.

"Nah...they don't have to be," I said as Ed nodded his head and gave Gail another hug.

"Are you in a hurry?" Ed asked Gail.

"Not really, I was on my way to South Street to buy some CDs."

"It must be karma!" I said excitedly.

"Great! We're on our way to Essence. Let's go." Ed chanted in his take-charge manner.

Off to Essence

What a great feeling, as we marched down Walnut Street. It was like old times, except the three of us now talked about our children, divorces, the passing of loved ones and friends, cholesterol counts, fiber supplements, colonoscopies, exercise, diet and other related topics instead of what classes we were going to take next semester, what careers we were planning, where our next group trip would be, whose house the next party was at, and the funny things our parents and siblings did at home. Ah, the joys of aging.

We laughed at old jokes and situations and expressed our sympathies about sad occurrences that each of us had experienced in our lives. It was as close to a perfect gathering of longtime friends as possible.

The three of us decided to stop at the music store first. The place was gigantic with three floors of CDs, vinyl records and videos. Even during this mid-week day in the mid-afternoon the store was crowded.

Gail had a list that included Celtic Music, Bob Marley, Dave Mason, Mozart, Dean Martin and The Dixie Chicks. Good range of tastes I thought as we helped her find the titles. With her impulse buying habit in full swing, Gail wound up purchasing a dozen CDs.

"Are you planning an extended solitary confinement period or haven't you gone music shopping in a very long time?" I asked with a bit of friendly sarcasm.

"There's a good explanation, I just bought myself a new Saab with a six

CD changer and wanted to stock it with some of the music that I listen to on my turntable...yes guys I still have a turntable and lots of albums. But since I can't hook up my turntable to the cigarette lighter I figured I better get into the 21st century and get some CDs."

"Whew, you must be the last vinyl holdout," Ed said in disbelief.

"Yep, guess I am...it's the music purist in me. I still like the Dead, the Beatles, The Stones, The Moody Blues and all those other groups we used to listen to way into the night on the thing we used to listen to 'em on. Reckon it's just me!"

"You don't stand there and watch the label go round and round like you used to during those all night parties, do you Gail?"

"Ok, that's it! Enough Sir Chazworth!" Gail exclaimed in mock anger.

As we walked down the eastern end of South Street I watched a mosaic of people pass by the restaurants, clothing boutiques, book shops, art galleries and stores selling everything from music and memorabilia to tattoos and tee shirts. The street is a microcosm of America. Every ethnic, age and income group is represented. And all the religions, sexual preferences and lifestyles are mixed together in a fantastic quilt of humanity that reflects the diversity of a great city. Even on this weekday the street was teeming with humanity. Tourists and residents, townies (the name Philadelphians use for people who live in Center City) and suburbanites stride side-by-side while retirees walk next to young people who talk on their cell phones as others zip by on skateboards. Women holding hands with women, men holding hands with men, share the sidewalk with "traditional" couples who are also clasping each other's hands or clutching each other's waists. Artists, lawyers, musicians, teachers, mechanics and restaurant workers are all talking, singing and shopping to the humming beat of humanity. The energy on the street is intense.

On to Fourth Street

The three of us make a right turn off of South Street, which leads us onto Fourth Street. Together we all release a harmonious sigh as we move onto a quieter venue. Even though there are restaurants on the street, they are surrounded by fabric shops and residences, real estate and notary offices.

The energy level is so different on Fourth Street that it reminds me of the change in decibel level I experience when I sit in my living room and the heater, which had been running in the background without my conscious knowledge, stops and all of a sudden I recognize a new silence that seems to suck out the noise that was making up the unconscious backdrop of my previous state of existence.

Gail informs us that she might retire next year and turn her avocation into a vocation by becoming a travel writer for a magazine in the city, a job she had already been offered.

"Sounds like a toast is in order?" is my reply as we reach our destination.

The three of us enter Essence and walk through the store/café in search of our mid-afternoon snack. Glistening displays of organic vegetables greet us. Off to the left are rows of mangoes, oranges, peaches and nectarines and other "regular" and exotic edible delights. Milk, soy products and frozen deserts are in the refrigerated section to our right. The publications, bulk cereals and nuts and snack areas are behind us as are the tables and chairs. The place smells like a combination of fruits, grains and the clean scent of the pages of a freshly printed book.

We each order a fruit smoothie drink from the attractive young African-American woman behind the counter. Her long pulled-back dreadlocks remind me of the picture of Bob Marley on the cover of the CD that Gail purchased a few minutes earlier; and her pierced lip, eyebrow and nose impress me as an artistic expression of her generation. She proceeds to throw strawberries, blueberries, raspberries, a bit of soy milk and ice into a blender. I pay for the smoothies, leave a tip and bring the three drinks over to the table next to the front window where Gail and Ed are already seated.

Ed raises his cardboard cup and proceeds with a toast. "To Gail, may you travel much, write well and have one continuous hell of a time...in safety, fun and prosperity!"

"Here, here!" was all I could think of.

Ed said "Where?" and Gail said "Merci, you fine gentlemen...now let's drink!"

After a few gulps of our smoothies Ed begins to talk about the conversation he and I had earlier in the day about energy and Ruth and tuning into frequencies.

Gail stopped Ed in mid-sentence. "I remember Ruth. And I remember all three of us talking about that episode for quite a while back then. But do you remember the time that we were at a party and Joan Crozen was laying in a bed sleeping and you said that you were going to try to mentally communicate with her. You told me that if you concentrated enough you could send energy from the middle of your forehead to the middle of hers and send thoughts from your mind to hers. Whew...that was outrageous! It was so weird because we were standing and she was lying down on her right side facing us and when she opened her eyes and said that the middle of her forehead felt really hot I almost fell over!"

"I do remember that," Ed said. "And I remember thinking how cool it would be if everyone learned a technique that would enable them to do that on an as wanted basis."

"I must have been in another room, don't ya think?" I added.

"I guess, 'cause it would have been strange if you weren't with us," Gail acknowledged as she went on. "I'll tell you something else that initially freaked me out, but once it kept happening I just got used to it. I'll never forget us driving around and you singing and while you were croonin' away I'd turn on the radio and lo and behold the song you were singing was on. At first I thought that it was a coincidence but it happened so many times that it couldn't have been. And it didn't only happen with the radio, it happened with conversations. It was like you knew what the people were gonna say before they said it. I remember us talking about it, but refresh my memory. What the heck was that about? And can you still do it?"

"It was about concentrating your energy and being open to receive incoming energy as well. Do you think that the only things that can receive sound, radio, television or any other kind of waves are just the instruments that were built to receive them? Or do you think that it's possible for some other vehicle to intercept those waves or pick up those waves in addition to the item that was built for that purpose? Ponder this, if a million radios can pick up the same signal why can't someone's mind act as a receiver as well and be number one million and one?"

"It makes sense now that you put it in that context." Gail answered, as I nodded my head in agreement.

"So if that's the case – we must all be walking receivers," I chimed in.

"Of course!" Ed replied "You're receiving my words right now because you're tuned into what I'm saying, or sending out. But don't you think it's possible to tune into something else, something not in our normal realm and pick up on that? All the energy that's being sent out in this room has a receiver somewhere and if you open up to it it's very possible that you can pick up on some of those waves as well. And I have to tell you that when we'd be driving in one of our cars, more often then not, weather I was the one at the wheel or somebody else was...I'd remove my self from myself and hover above, while still inside the car enjoying our conversations. And when we'd all walk down Vernon Road near your house Gail, I'd be watching us walk from above the trees. It's so vivid. I remember seeing that neon sign that spelled out Flick's Deli and how we'd joke about how the letters used to blend together to spell out an entirely different word." Gail and I nodded our heads and laughed without taking our eyes off of

Ed. "And" Ed added, "How I would look at it from down the block and above as we all strolled down the street."

Ed continued: "During the time that I went through all the experiences we've been talking about I used to lie in bed in the evening and see the energy patterns in the air. I'd tilt my head and look across the room and see the dancing waves or I'd look up at the ceiling and see the energy vibrating. What a gas! I was one totally open receiver! It was a fantastic time that continued for years, then my business started to get really busy and I diverted my energy. My business focus became so extreme that I lost a greater, and what I think now was a more important, focus. But I've come full circle. So I guess it was supposed to happen that way."

"What do you mean full circle?" I asked.

"Like I said when we met in the park earlier today Chaz, it's finally come together over the past year."

"Am I going to have the pleasure of your knowledge today or am I gonna have to wait?" Gail questioned, with a mixed expression of excitement and disappointment.

"It'll be tough to get it all in at one sitting but let's keep goin' and who knows!" Ed responded as he rose up from his chair to get a few more napkins.

Viewenics

Returning to the table, Ed started to speak again. "Years ago at Community College we had a yogi come and speak to us. It was during the time that I was going through all my experiences and after my situation with Ruth. I can still see him sitting in the lotus position on the stage that was set up in the cafeteria. As I stood along the right side of the stage and a few rows back in the audience I could see a yellow-gold aura emanating from this man who seemed to be calm and at rest. He was dressed in his white linen outfit that included a loose fitting shirt and drawstring pants. His hair was black and very long and I can recall that he was wearing a necklace of beige and brown beads.

"It was the first time I had been able to witness someone's aura. And it wasn't until some time later that I learned that a yellow-gold aura was the sign of a highly powerful and developed spiritual teacher.

"Seeing his aura, and recounting my own incidences, including others that I'll get to, made me wonder even more about my ability to leave my body and watch the world as if it was a movie that I was in," Ed continued.

"After doing all that research and still not coming up with a totally viable explanation, I began to realize that perhaps the reason I couldn't find a word to describe my experiences was because no one had categorized it in a manner that would enable it to have one. So, I set about thinking of a word that would capture the separation of the spiritual self from the physical self while still being connected to each other."

As Ed spoke I could feel myself being drawn into his every word. I glanced over at Gail and saw that she had begun to lean so far forward towards Ed that the tips of her hair were about to take a smoothie bath. I motioned to her to move her locks out of the puree. She complied by taking out a rubber band from her purse and haphazardly tying her hair back without diverting her attention from Ed.

"I decided to call it *Viewenics,*" Ed went on, "a combination of the ability to view one's surroundings from a broader perspective, while understanding that it incorporates energy and is based in the principles of physics.

"The phrase, 'out of body experience,' just didn't capture the full essence of the knowledge I had gained. As the days passed, I noticed that I could, in fact, remove my 'self' from my body at will. I could stand back and look at myself, and how I interacted with my environment. It gave me an energy flow that was free and open.

"Through all these years I have chronicled my *Viewenic* experiences in my diary, this little book that I always carry with me. Every few days I photocopy the most recently written pages...like backing up documents on a computer.

"And now it's time."

As Ed said that, Gail and I looked at each other with a bit of excitement coupled with extreme curiosity.

What do you mean, "And now it's time?" I asked.

"Well, do you remember earlier today I said that it's finally come together, and I know what I'm supposed to do on this earth," Ed said directing his question towards me.

"Yes I do...and you said something about helping people in Lithuania and then changed it to Latvia," I said with a bit of sarcasm mixed in with a touch of respect, as Gail looked on quizzically. "And, I added, you never did get around to answering me!"

"Hmmm...guess you're right Chazo. I was probably waiting for the planets to align and send us Gail!" He responded with a glowing smile and a seated upper torso slight swagger.

Walking to the Car

Gail seemed quite flattered by the suggestion that Ed might have actually waited to reveal his mission in life only after encountering our long lost friend.

"Before I let you in on my life's task, there are a few things that I have to tell you both. Earlier, I told you that the reason I stopped having *Viewenic* experiences was because my business began to divert my energy.

That's true – but only partially. You see I also consciously stopped them because of occurrences that happened with Sam Baum, capped off by one situation with him in particular. You both remember Sam, right?"

"Sure." Both Gail and I said in unison.

Sam was a slim, curly haired fellow. He was very intellectual and reminded me of Art Garfunkel, of Simon & Garfunkle, same kind of hair and build...but not the same kind of voice!

"And what was that occurrence, Ed?" Gail asked as the hair that hadn't quite made it into the rubber band was now firmly planted in her smoothie.

"Let me step back and tell you about a few other situations that happened previous to the main episode with Sam."

Both Gail and I let out a "Why?" only to have Ed respond by telling us how integral the situations were to the major Sam story to follow.

Then Ed said, "How 'bout we head out and take a ride?"

"Huh? Now?" I responded. "Why argue Chaz?" Gail said with a chuckle. "We've got all day. Why not enjoy everything about it?"

Gail wiped her hair down with a wet napkin, laughed and said, "Well, I'm clean…so let's go!" as she tossed the damp paper into the trash can next to the door.

The three of us left Essence and walked past the shops and restaurants on 4th Street, we crossed South Street as we all commented on the mellow tones of a saxophone being played in front of a vintage clothing store. We continued to walk north towards Lombard Street while we talked about the preponderance of coffee houses in the city, raising our voices over the din of other people talking and cars slowly making their way down 4th while others idled on South Street as they waited for the stoplight to change to green.

A woman with closely cropped jet black hair, bright red lipstick, a pink tank top with the words "I BREAK FOR PEACE" on the back, royal blue high top sneakers and a pair of baggy black jeans, was walking about three or four steps in front of us discussing her love for Salvador Dali's works with her male companion. He was attired in a Philadelphia Eagles baseball cap worn backwards, a very loose fitting blue and yellow plaid shirt, baggy khakis, and very clunky big brown shoes.

They seemed to agree on how inspiring his works were to their own artwork when the woman lifted her left arm and said, "Look what I just got!" It was a tattoo of one of Dali's famous *Soft Watches* – from his painting, *The Persistence of Memory*. The young man was beside himself with joy! They suddenly stopped as they laughed and jumped up and down and hugged each other.

We pardoned ourselves and asked for a peek. It was, I must admit, quite a nice piece of artwork on its own. Gail and Ed felt the same as we thanked the couple and made our way north, debating whether or not any of us would ever get a tattoo. The consensus was no…but we all admitted that they certainly were interesting to look at and many of them were rather attractive.

As we approached Lombard Street with its colonial homes, we passed a schoolyard where elementary school kids were giggling and yelling, jumping on jungle gyms and playing dodge ball. What a great sound, probably my favorite, the sound of kids laughing. There's something about it that brings a warm, calming and satisfying feeling deep inside me and brings a smile to my face. We made a left on Pine Street and walked by St. Peter's Church and the graveyard that's been there since the 1700's.

When we turned right onto 5th Street Ed began to get back into the topic we were so interested in. He started by talking about his father.

A Father's Insight and Soul

"When I was a young boy, about nine or ten, my father would talk to me about the future. One day he said that men would grow their hair really long and wear earrings, they'd wear high-heeled shoes and brightly colored clothes, pants that would have one leg in one color and the other leg a different color. Then he said we'd be able to see the other person we were speaking to when we spoke on the phone. These things stuck in my mind from that point forward. And, you all know that that's exactly what started to happen ten years later. Guys started to grow their hair longer, wear earrings, wear those high-heeled platform boots and shoes, and wear every color under the sun. What really struck me was when I went to a concert and saw some fella wearing a pair of pants that had one leg that was red and the other yellow! It blew my mind. Now... video phones, video conferencing and video e-mails are pretty common. So, I guess my dad was ahead of his time...if he could only be here walking with us now. But in some manner I know he is," Ed said with a bit of melancholy in his voice.

"There was something spiritual about my dad, even though he was not religious at all, he seemed to connect with people and their needs, understand what was truly right and wrong, and convey his feelings with a passion that made people see things in a different light. He knew what energy could do."

"You're right Ed. I always had that feeling when I spoke with your dad. He just knew how to relate to people on a core level," Gail interjected.

"Wise, I believe the word is," I said as we passed Spruce Street and arrived back on Walnut.

There, staring us in the face was a beautiful palomino horse that shook his head as if to greet us as we crossed at the corner to continue our march towards Gail's car. He was pulling a carriage filled with a family of six. I could hear the driver, who was attired in colonial garb, explaining to the people how the Founding Fathers walked these streets and what it looked like during those times. Ah history, I love it, I thought.

"When my father died I was with him." Ed continued "Right before he passed away I viewed us together; him laying on his bed and me sitting next to the bed on a chair, from the ceiling of his hospital room. This was five years after my first experience and quite a while after I consciously stopped because of my encounter with Sam. The very moment that my dad passed, I was no longer viewing us from above. I was seated again and I saw his soul leave his body and rise above him."

The three of us were no longer walking, we stopped and Gail and I looked at Ed. He seemed to be reliving the moment as if he was there.

"You saw your dad's soul?" I asked rhetorically. "What was it like?"

"It was like heat rising up from his body but more in the shape of a candle's flame, just much wider and not pointed like a candle's flame...I instantly knew that it was his soul.

"You see guys...that's why I'm sure we have a soul or everlasting energy or a connection with the rest of everything there is, whatever you want to call it, because I've seen it and I know it's there," Ed remarked.

"And I know that my dad's still with me as well as my other loved ones who have passed away, just like your loved ones are there for you. They're just in a different form and dimension. They're no longer mass, but they certainly are energy." He added.

Gail and I were speechless for a few seconds.

After thinking about what Ed had said I replied, "It makes sense that when we die our life energy has to go somewhere, and like you said – it doesn't disappear. So, the frequency that it's on must enable it to transcend to another place."

"I believe you understand Chaz," Ed responded

"Which means that everything we've heard our religious leaders say about our souls must be right after all?" Gail added

"Not exactly Gail...not everything. I think that that may be where our concepts have become a little skewed, which brings me back to Sam," Ed stated.

"You see, one thing that we as humans have become very good at is filtering everything through our values and beliefs systems, even what happens to us and our energy. And that creates judgmental reactions and a hazy view of what actually is. I tried to explain that to Sam."

Taking a Ride

"Here we are!" Gail exclaimed. "My Car, what a parking spot…and 10 minutes left on the meter to boot!"

She had parked her car on Walnut Street about a block west of Independence Hall.

"Hey Gail, how come you didn't tell us you were parked at a meter. We would've left earlier," I asked.

"I guess I must have known that it wouldn't be a problem. Probably that connective energy, plus I will assume that you guys must have picked up the vibration," she said with a wink and a smile.

As we got into the car, a black late model Audi pulled up next to us, and the driver asked if we were leaving. We told him we were and he thanked us with a wave and a nod. Parking spaces in downtown Philly are hard to find.

Off we drove, up Walnut Street from 6th to 16th Street, past all the people and high-end stores and restaurants. We went from, what many folks consider the historic area to the financial and business district – however, there are plenty of both in each.

Sitting in the car with Ed and Gail brought back so many memories that I felt that I had flashed back to the late '60s or early '70s. We were together again, ahhh…what a great feeling! We were laughing, singing along as we listened to the oldies station on the radio, and kidding each other about things we did many years ago.

"Go up the Parkway, please," Ed requested of Gail. "No Problem," was her reply. The Parkway is actually named the Benjamin Franklin Parkway.

It's an incredibly beautiful thoroughfare that was designed much like the Champs Elysees in Paris. Its wide inner drive is six lanes and its narrower outer drives are two lanes each. At one end of the Parkway is City Hall, the tallest masonry building in the world, with a statue of William Penn atop it. His statue is the largest one to grace the top of any building anywhere. The Hall is an attraction in its own right. There are an amazing number of intricately sculpted figures gracing the building, all designed by the same renowned man who designed the statue of William Penn, Alexander Milne Calder. And right before City Hall is Love Park, the place once famous for its skateboarders as well as its Robert Indiana LOVE statue. The skate boarders are gone, but the sculpture is still there.

Gail takes us past Chestnut, Market, and Arch Streets and past JFK Boulevard and makes a left onto the Parkway. What an amazing sight it is. No matter how many times I drive down the Parkway its beauty always awes me. This time of year the Parkway is in full bloom. Flowers color the already magnificent scenery like a giant Monet painting. Yellows, reds, whites, purples, pinks and lavenders and just about every other hue that nature affords us, mix with the greens of the grasses and the leaves of the trees. And from all the street lamps on the inner drive, perpendicular to the street, hang the flags of the counties of the world. Today, they flap gently in the warm breeze. All of them seem to sparkle in the sunlight. Everyone in alphabetical order save Israel, which holds the position of the first flag, as you enter the road from 16th Street, because it is next to the monument to the Six Million Jewish Martyrs, the Jews who died at the hands of the Nazis during the Second World War.

The Parkway is filled with monuments and fountains. There, in front of us, is a piece of my family's legacy. The Swann Fountain on Logan Circle – with its incredible statuary, sculpted by the famous Alexander Stirling Calder (son of Alexander Milne Calder)...the water spouting swans, turtles and frogs, its majestic Native Americans and other equally compelling people, along with its awesome landscaping, all reach out to me each time I see it. It is a point of pride for everyone related to me that my grandfather built that fountain. He was an engineer and he and his company worked with the sculptors and designers to fashion one of the city's most beautiful attractions.

We drive around Logan Circle and now see the Parkway in its full visual splendor. At its end is the Philadelphia Museum of Art, sitting on the top of a hill and looking like the Parthenon as it surveys the skyline. The Art Museum is now known as much for the film character Rocky's race up its steps as it is for its majesty and collections.

Gail's medium blue Toyota Camry heads towards the right, past one of the two monolithic monuments dedicated to the union sailors and soldiers of the Civil War and onto the inner drive. We travel past more statues, monuments, outstanding landscaping and buildings. Then Ed tells Gail to find a parking space near the Rodin Museum.

Sitting by Rodin

Gail has her parking karma intact and gets a space right in front of the place. She only needs to back the car into the spot once to pull off a parking miracle, the perfect space and the perfect park job.

Out we tumble laughing about Gail's karmic abilities and her lucky park job. Ed comments that it was the first time he ever saw Gail park with less than eight or ten back and forth maneuvers in order to fit securely into a space without sticking her car halfway into the street or on the curb.

Gail retaliates by taking her Philadelphia Inquirer out of her handbag and mockingly slapping it across Ed's arm. Unfortunately for her and us, the entire newspaper comes apart and begins to make its way up and down the pavement in the spring breeze. Like the Keystone Cops of the old silent movies, the three of us hunt down the sheets of newsprint, tripping over each other as we run around chasing the elusive pages, one of which is caught in the wake of a passing Mazda and gets lifted up in the turbulence only to plant itself firmly on Ed's face. He pries at it as if passing through a spider web while Gail and I double over in laughter and inadvertently smash our heads into each other. We are now three walking wounded trying to make our way the hundred or so feet to the entrance of the Rodin Museum while attempting to gently assemble the Inquirer back to its original form.

The museum, bordering on 22nd Street, faces the Parkway and Gail's car.

It is set a sizable distance back from the sidewalk and if you're traveling quickly you may not notice its grandeur. But once you take the time and move up towards its entrance, the first thing you see is Rodin's most well-known piece, The Thinker. The museum, a gift of the late local philanthropist and theater mogul Jules Mastbaum, has the largest collection of the master's works outside of Paris and draws admirers from around the world, yet its quiet elegance and humble stature almost belie what one finds inside and out.

We move around The Thinker as if doing some sort of strange courtship dance. Three bees around a flower enthralled with its lines, character, beauty and intensity. Ed finally moves us along to the entrance of the building. We stand in amazement as we notice the two giant doors immediately in front of us. Within seconds I realize that these doors are not the entrance to the museum but a sculpture attached to its exterior. The actual entrances are to either side of 'The Gates of Hell.' The 'Gates' do not open, and were never meant to. On it are miniatures of some of Rodin's full-size pieces, including 'The Thinker' and 'The Kiss' along with many of his other incredible works, some gruesome, some intriguing, all astounding. The Master's masterpiece took more then 15 years to finish. We stand and gaze. We are mesmerized.

Ed breaks the silence and reminds us of his philosophy that heaven and hell are constructs; inventions of our minds, fantasies intertwined with our value systems, perceptions that many have turned into realities that they use to guide their behavior.

Ed moved back down towards the building's lawn and beckoned Gail and I to sit with him in an area in front of the museum. We choose a spot on the grass within view of 'The Gates of Hell' and 'The Thinker' and sprawl ourselves out like we did when we saw Jimmy Hendrix, Country Joe and the Fish, and The Grateful Dead in concert at Temple University Stadium in our old neighborhood.

"Just like old times," I said as Ed and Gail nodded their heads in agreement.

"Yep, old times and new times…they have somehow flowed together in a whisper of time, and here we are," Ed reasoned and resumed.

"I decided to come here to continue telling you about Sam and all the other things that relate to my new decisions because of "The Thinker," which symbolizes something we should all do if we're gonna move to more enlightened levels of consciousness and to look at 'The Gates of Hell,' which illustrates how people allow themselves to become engrossed in realistic fantasies that can remove them from what is and what may be.

"Our value systems and our beliefs help dictate our thoughts and perceptions and that is what, I believe, happened to Sam with reference to how he viewed me. Ed Elias is who I am and was, and yet he had a different feeling.

"Back at Community College when we all did the school paper, I remember walking into the newspaper office up on the second floor across from the lounge. About the fifth or sixth time I walked in, Sam said to me that every time he or someone else in the place mentioned Jesus I entered the office. Well…I thought, I'm not gonna touch that one. Sam, I said… that's just a coincidence and intentionally shrugged it off. I could see and feel what was coming and I wasn't comfortable with it. Not even a little bit. And – he repeated it to me on a couple of occasions."

"You're kidding." Gail exclaimed.

"I wish I was…but it's the truth," Ed said in what seemed like a continuation of years of disbelief.

"And he was with us throughout so many of your experiences," I added.

"Yeah, I know, but that's not the entire story.

"In between the newspaper office situations and the time of my last discussion with Sam, the one that made me consciously stop my *Viewenic* experiences, a number of other things happened."

Laughter and Vision

Gail and I were now glued to Ed's words. He repositioned himself from the sprawled state we were all in, to sitting straight up while assuming a half lotus position. The posture would have almost given him the look of a yogi if it wasn't for the 'I Like Ike' pin that somehow had manifested itself on his tee shirt. A smiling President Eisenhower had diverted my attention and serious thought. There was something about Ed that made the incongruity bizarre yet not out of character. I had to stop the conversation.

"How did an Ike button appear on your tee shirt without us seeing it before?" I questioned

Gail was laughing so uncontrollably that I was sure she would revisit her smoothie.

"Why do you do that, Ed?" I demanded, holding back my own laughter.

"Because, once we start taking ourselves too seriously…it's over," he replied. "To some degree, that's my point! Oh yeah – and I put it on when we were walking over to this spot from 'The Gates of Hell.' And remember; always carry an 'I Like Ike' pin in your pocket for times like these."

Gail wiped the tears of laughter from her eyes while I shook my head in mock disbelief.

Ed continued, "Ok, where were we? Oh yeah…I'd like you both to think back and let me know if you remember this particular night. We were all invited to a party in Center City. I know the three of us were there along with Alan, Victor, Joan, Olga Podiak, Tanya Nikkie, and a couple of other people from our group. We started out the evening at somebody's apartment across the street from the main party. I think we were there to pick someone up before we went to the other place. Anyhow, I remember sitting on the floor of the first apartment next to the coffee table talking to Olga and Tanya who were also sitting on the floor, they were across from me, next to the couch and leaning against the coffee table. All of a sudden while we were conversing I heard a voice inside me say, 'The Jews are coming, the Jews are coming.' It was so odd, but I can recall the moment those phrases were spoken like it was 5 minutes ago. I half-heartedly shrugged it off while at the same time it stayed in my mind.

"Shortly after I heard the voice, we got up and walked across the street to the other apartment and the party. The place was pretty crowded and as Olga, Tanya and I continued our conversation we made our way through the living room and stopped next to the window on the far side of the apartment. I distinctly remember standing perpendicular to the window and the outside wall that faced the street; both were to my right. The kitchen was about three yards in front of me and the living room was to my left. There were quite a few people in the faintly lit kitchen and a few more in the living room. A large pink and blue neon sign was flashing across the street and its reflection sent the colors into the apartment, intermittently tinting the walls with its soft hues.

"As Olga, Tanya and I kept up our conversation I was standing crossed legged discussing something when I spread my arms out wide to illustrate a point, and for some reason I also closed my eyes. All of a sudden I was no longer in that apartment. Instead, I was on the top of a mountain looking down on tens of thousands of people. I felt serenity, calmness, wisdom, enlightenment, compassion, and peace, not only emanating from me but from the people below as well. As I viewed the enormous crowd I could also see that there was bright red blood on my hands and a sizeable amount of blood on my shirt as well. It formed a spot the size of my fully extended hand on the middle left side of my chest.

"The amount of time that my eyes were closed could have been a millisecond or a million years. It was literally timeless.

"I really don't know how long I stood in that position but what I do know is that Olga's scream quickly brought me back to the apartment. She was freaking out. I asked her what was wrong. She was hysterical. I took her by the hand, led her and Tanya into the living room and asked them to sit on the couch. I knelt on the floor, on my right knee, in front of the couch, held onto Olga's hand and again asked her why she had gotten so emotional. She replied that she saw blood on my shirt and hands while she was speaking with me. Olga then went on to say that the blood just appeared and she saw it on the chest of my shirt and on the palms of my hands and that the blood was fresh and slowly flowing out of wounds. She was repeating everything exactly as I had seen it, not unlike what Victor had done when he and I had our experience in Alan's apartment."

"You know, I do remember being there. And I also remember Olga's scream. But I didn't recall the reason," Gail said as I added, "Me too."

"The reason you don't recall why she screamed was because I asked both her and Tanya not to say anything. I just told people that everything was ok.

"I didn't want everyone asking questions and interpreting the answers."

Gail and I were totally engrossed by Ed's revelation.

"I didn't even tell Olga and Tanya that I had experienced exactly what they had related. I just listened and said that it may have been the lighting or the way I was standing. Olga, of course felt differently but I made light of it, allayed her fears, said something to make them laugh and changed the subject. The night went on without any further incidences.

"It was shortly thereafter that Sam and I had our now famous encounter.

"I don't know if Olga or Tanya had spoken with Sam or if he derived at his conclusion himself, but it happened nonetheless."

I Know Who You Are

"It was a few weeks later and again…as usual, we were at a party in somebody's house. The regular group was there, including Sam. As he and I spoke he said to me, 'I know who you are.'

"I responded by asking him to come with me so that we could sit down and discuss what he said," Ed continued as Gail and I looked at each other with a combination of disbelief and anticipation.

"I know what you told him Ed," I interjected trying to be funny. "You told him that he found you out and that you were really the reincarnation of Babe Ruth and you were about to send him over the wall like a well placed pitch if he didn't straighten out!"

Both Ed and Gail groaned at my poor attempt at humor.

"No, Chaz…that's not exactly what happened," Ed deadpanned.

"Sam and I went into another room by ourselves. We sat on the floor cross-legged, next to each other at a forty-five degree angle. The room was relatively dark, except that behind Sam there was light coming through what I think was a window shade that had been pulled down to the floor. It actually looked more like a backlit rectangular drumhead that emanated a fairly bright whitish blue light from behind it. Sam was silhouetted against the backdrop. I can still see the outline of his body and particularly his hair, which was in its usual naturally frizzed-out style."

"Ed," he said right after he sat down, "I really do know who you are."

"Do you Sam?" was my reply. "Yes Ed, you're Jesus Christ."

Gail and I couldn't believe what we were hearing, although I think we each knew what Sam was going to say.

"*That's* when I told him that I was really Babe Ruth!" Ed said breaking the seriousness of the moment.

"Well guys, as you can imagine, I was quite taken aback by Sam's statement. Even though I knew it was coming. However, I immediately responded by telling Sam that we all contained elements of Jesus, Moses, even Hitler, as well as every great and not so great individual who has inhabited and/or continues to inhabit this Earth. We all have their capabilities within us, and that he was as much Jesus as I was.

"I also think that because my long hair and the rest of my physical being had that look that so many people associate with Jesus it added to his concept, even though scholars agree that he didn't look like that at all. In those days the Jews of that locale had short hair, which tended to be wavy or curly and they were more olive skinned as the people of the Middle East are today. In fact the images we have of Jesus today really come from impressions closer to that of Alexander The Great.

"Anyway…it was shortly thereafter that I consciously decided to stop my *Viewenic* experiences.

"I realized that Sam was looking for someone to follow rather than looking inward, and I certainly didn't want or need an ego trip like that!

"There should be no ego in any of this. Especially since we all have the same capacity to experience what was happening to me. It was important to me to make sure that Sam understood that I didn't have any special 'powers.' As I sat there I kept thinking and saying, 'Sam, please realize that if you just harness the energy within you, everything that you witnessed happening to me will happen to you.'

"But it was to no avail, he wanted to project his beliefs onto me. He wanted to follow as opposed to being a leader…a leader in a land of leaders.

"I really felt that when I saw myself on top of that mountain I wasn't anyone special. I just felt as if I was someone who had realized a gift that we all have, including the people below. I will say however…that the view was spectacular, as all my *Viewenic* views are. And, that I also believed that I was looking at people who were from a land of leaders, people leading themselves while taking in and sending out love for and from everyone."

Culture and Experiences

"I thought extensively about my sit-down with Sam and I understood that part of the reason that Sam related me to Jesus and even I related my experience with Olga to Jesus, or someone being crucified, the Jews, that time period and types of spiritual beings and situations, was that that's what being brought up in a Judeo-Christian culture has taught me to do. If I was brought up in the Hindu religion I might have experienced Shiva or Krishna, if I was a Buddhist it would have been Buddha or if I was brought up as a Muslim I may have encountered Mohammed...as Sam would have.

"Understanding that was as much of an epiphany as the experiences themselves. I really wanted Sam to comprehend that it wasn't about me. It was about him. He was Jesus, Moses or whoever he wanted me to be. He could experience what I had experienced. I knew how important it was for him to know that he had all the 'powers' that he thought only I had. It was just that I had been fortunate enough to have manifested them... that's it, nothing more or less.

"But he didn't realize that. He really thought that I was Jesus. Interestingly enough he became a Messianic Jew after that...and I stopped having anything to do with *Viewenics*, at least for a while. Could you imagine? Whenever I see people professing to be a profit or a divine being, it makes me sad for the people who follow them and perturbed at the people who portray themselves as greater or more privileged, in whatever way, than their followers. All people have to do is realize that we all have it…every single one of us."

Gail and I were emotionally spent. I felt like I had gone through a life altering experience. Gail sat there staring at Ed as if under a spell.

Ed went on. "Until recently, I didn't think that I would climb back on the horse. I've had other experiences, but kept them to myself. Now I know how important it is to relate to people how much more there is to their spirits, their minds, their abilities to learn, soar, grow and love. Instead of realizing that my discussion with Sam was just a discussion with one person who interpreted his experiences with me from his perspective, I should have addressed his thoughts and given him additional perspectives from my view, and reinforced them extensively. In addition, I allowed it to be interpreted by me as something that could turn into an ego trip fueled by Sam, with the possibility of him enlisting others. That's exactly the opposite of what I knew it should be.

"I saw an ugly side and stopped, knowing full well how so many situations like that have lead to too many terrible things."

"I have one question though Ed," Gail said in a tone that seemed to come from deep inside her mind. "How can you explain the fact that Olga saw the same blood, in the same positions on your body that you saw?"

"Interesting that you should ask me that Gail," Ed responded "Because I thought about that quite a bit after the event. She was seeing what I was projecting. The energy that I was sending out and her receiver were on the same frequency. It just happened that at that time I was projecting what I was experiencing and she had the ability to see it. To put a religious significance on it takes away from our capacity to bring it into our everyday world. *Viewenics* and spirituality are different from religion, they're within us, like blood, thoughts, water, and oxygen, and they are not to be confused with religion. Why do people so often think that only other, more important people, as they conceive them, have those abilities? Why? That's how they get controlled, manipulated, and subservient. What was Sam's perception of himself to have him get to that conclusion? For that matter, what can anyone's perception of themselves be to enable them to think that they have less capacities and capabilities than anyone else?

"This brings me to the realization of what I'm supposed to do with the rest of my time on this Earth and maybe beyond it," Ed said as he first looked at me with a slight smile and then turned his eyes towards Gail.

Waiting for This Moment

This was the moment I had been waiting for since our discussion earlier in the day.

"But first I have a question for both of you," Ed said knowing full well that we were in anticipation of the revelation of his life's purpose.

"How good can the teacher, even the ultimate teacher, be if his or her students always remain the students and the teacher always remains the teacher?"

"Very provocative question Ed," was Gail's reply.

"This isn't one of those trick questions where the answer is a number, is it?" I asked in mock seriousness. "Forty-one…forty-one – that my dear friend is the answer," I proclaimed.

"Ok, you're right…forty-one it is. Let's go for a soft pretzel," Ed said as he began to get up from his quasi-lotus position.

"Stop it!" Gail yelled half smiling, "Both of you…stop it now!"

"Yes Ms. Carlow," Ed said in a tone reflecting that of a student in a high school class.

"I guess there has to come a time when the student and teacher begin to switch roles, parts, or get on an equal plane with each other," Gail said as she answered Ed's question.

"Or do all of those on a continuous basis," I added.

"Exactly…here's the thing," Ed interjected, as he looked at us with that 'get ready for some deep stuff' expression. "It's kind of like when someone's been seeing a therapist for ten years. When is enough, enough? Doesn't there have to come a time when the patient is 'cured' and if, after ten years, he or she isn't, shouldn't they find another therapist?"

"When people spend a disproportionate amount of time looking for answers about their lives and life in general from others, reliance develops and that person then becomes dependent on answers from without rather then taking the time to learn and form their decisions from within.

"If the teacher is a guide, someone who points them in a direction, rather than telling them that this is where they are, and need to be, the student can discover new vistas on his or her own. The teacher helps but doesn't control. That enables the student to have a map and make the discoveries on his or her own, which is far more enthralling and much easier to absorb. And, it also allows the student to teach the teacher new things.

"So you see, in that way, after a short period of time, the teacher becomes the student and the student becomes the teacher and the process flows back and forth like a pendulum on a continuum.

"My friends…that is my mission in life, to teach and learn, and learn and teach, and hopefully show others not to get caught up in the need to be controlled or the need to control, not to look for idols but to look for knowledge, because the greatest idol is yourself and the greatest gifts are energy and its beautiful by-product, love. But that's not for me to force on you, it's only for me to give you my thoughts about it and for you to discover and make the decision. I've told you about my *Viewenic* experiences. And I can tell you the processes to achieve *Viewenic* experiences on your own. But it's up to you to realize them, up to you to interpret them, up to you to teach others once you've learned them, and up to you to teach me the new things that you've discovered in order to enrich your life and mine as well.

"You see, after all these years, I recognized the fact that Sam taught me something. He made me understand that there are certain things that should be dispelled. I've realized over the years that the most spiritual individuals I've had the pleasure to interact with or learn about, really only wanted people to experience the energy of the universe in things like peace, wisdom and knowledge, contentment and compassion, health and prosperity, enlightenment and laughter, happiness and love. And I mean real love, love for our species and other species, love for our Earth and the universe, love of family and of mates and partners, deep romantic love and soft caring love. I don't believe that any spiritual person wants others to follow them to the point where the student gets lost in the teacher, what good would that do, how could an individual really grow? One thing I do know is that we need more spiritual people not people who follow spiritual people."

Separating Your Self from Yourself

"Once you separate your self from yourself and gain the *Viewenic* ability to see things from afar, you begin to understand how everything is related to everything else. You notice how hurting someone or something else means that you're ultimately hurting yourself. You can see and feel how all energy, and therefore everything, is interconnected. What purpose does it serve to take and not give, accept and not learn, teach and not understand, stifle your mind and not grow? These points, as timeless as some of them seem, are still not fully understood and experienced.

"I've gone on far too long my dear compadres," Ed concluded.

I felt clean, washed by a broader understanding of life. I also felt Gail's eyes on my face as I turned toward her. She had an expression that I hadn't seen on her in years. It was the calm expression of wisdom and peace. A combination of a slight tilt of the head to the right and the way one's lips curl up at the corners after they've tasted the perfect ice cream on a hot summer's day, the same expression that's usually accompanied by the sound…mmm. Complimenting her happy smile was a twinkle in her eyes as if she had just seen a humming bird gathering nectar from a honeysuckle. Her hands were together, palm to palm with the tops of her index fingers creating a resting place for her chin as she sat cross-legged on the soft, bright green grass.

"I get it." She said. "I understand what you have to do Chaz. And by listening to you today…what we all have to do in our own way."

"Thank you Gail," Ed replied humbly.

"It's our responsibility to learn, grow, understand, and pass on the knowledge so that others will do the same. You know that it's a circle. We lead by following and follow by leading. That's why everyone is involved. We're all equal and we all have the same abilities, none greater and none lesser. The energy is continuous. It's wonderful to know it and see it and pass it on and have others pass it on and back again to the original guide who then experiences something new for himself or herself," Ed added.

My senses seemed unusually heightened. The smell of the newly cut grass we are sitting on takes me back to a time in my childhood when my grandfather walked with me on our front lawn to examine the dogwood tree he had just planted. It was the same smell – fresh and clean, and it seemed that I was inside it; part of the sunlight, photosynthesis and the chlorophyll of each blade. The scent went straight into the part of my mind that unlocked the past. I smiled. I thought of him and saw him as he got down on his knees and compressed the fertilizer around the tree's base while telling me about the beautiful flowers that would bloom from its branches every spring. His straw fedora reflected the sunlight, his crisp white shirt, khaki pants and beige and brown spectator shoes made him look more like a man ready to attend a party flush with mint juleps and catfish than a proud homespun gardener showing his grandson his latest jewel. He spoke like a college professor yet he never graduated high school. He always inspired and amazed me. He was so successful and so humble. And then I realized that my recollections were part of what Ed was speaking about.

I had just experienced a view from above, a different kind of *Viewenic* event, but one nonetheless. I was lifted up both emotionally and spiritually. I saw myself and my grandfather, my home and lawn and all the surroundings. Was I really literally back in time? Was I a nine year old again? Yes, what other explanation could there be.

Our minds have the ability to take us to places that are timeless. I was there, most definitely.

I asked Ed, "Do you think that memories are *Viewenic* experiences?"

"Absolutely," he said and continued. "*Viewenics* is a function of our minds. It has depth and levels. My occurrence with Olga and Tanya were as much memories of situations that I had been conditioned to experience, as they were spontaneous. Memories of past events are multidimensional in nature. They can involve all our senses; just as current, unprompted and prompted *Viewenic* events can as well."

"So then, what prevents everyday life from being in a *Viewenic* state?" I asked.

"Perspective and closed receptors," Ed replied.

"You see, we as humans have let a fantastic ability slip away," Ed added. "*Viewenics*, while it's within each of us, too often goes untapped. We've clogged our minds with so much clutter that we have a tendency to think that the free flow of our own energy, the un-cluttering if you will, needs some special vehicle to enable us to do it. So we go on retreats and take classes, meditate and do yoga. And for most people who aspire to "free their minds" it works. The trick is to make it ongoing.

"When you've mastered *Viewenics* you've given real meaning to the term 'rise above it.' Isn't it amazing that that term is so often used without people really thinking about its meaning? It's the perfect *Viewenic* expression. Rise above it, literally, and you will understand that you are constantly meditating. With *Viewenics* you are living a yogic existence. It enables you to live horizontally and vertically at the same time. You can go through life on infinite planes, because you're tapping into the universal energy that's already there, just waiting to be experienced. All most people need in order to encounter it is a guide. And once they've achieved it they can become a guide for someone else, and the understanding and experiencing of *Viewenics* will grow with guides teaching and learning everywhere, so that everyone can become a spiritual guide. That would create an environment of inclusiveness and equality on a spiritual level not seen on this earth for a very long time, if ever. Everyone would be a leader! Imagine the energy!"

Ed was effusive in his speech. He seemed to be in tune with his message. His voice was flowing in harmony with the spring air. My understanding of his mission was becoming quite clear, as was my appreciation of *Viewenics* and its depths and levels. I had never contemplated memories in such an enlightened way. Or had I thought about meditation, yoga, and everyday experiences with such insight.

'Remove your self from yourself' and 'Rise above it' were now expressions that had much fuller meanings.

The Couple

Gail was looking towards the entrance of the Rodin Museum. Her eyes stared at a couple about fifteen feet away who were talking as they pointed to the flags on the Parkway.

She spoke without taking her eyes off the elderly man and woman. "You know Chaz; your dad once told me that meditation was a heck of a lot better than medication. And after listening to you Ed, I can really see his point."

"I had forgotten that he used to say that Gail. How right and wise he was!"

I was now also looking at the couple enjoying the array of flags. They seemed to be in their sixties or seventies. The man stood erect and was dressed in black jeans and white sneakers, his faded white tee shirt had a large blue peace sign on the front. His clean-shaven face displayed a soft smile as he ran his hand over his thinning gray hair to keep it in place. His eyes were large and light brown as was his complexion and he had a wide, prominent nose that gave his face a feeling of softness and kindness. He was about six feet tall and of medium build and looked as if he worked out on a regular basis.

His female companion was an attractive woman. She too wore black jeans. Her sky blue denim blouse bellowed in the breeze. She had gray hair that was long and flowing. I could see it reached her waist as she moved her head to look down the Parkway. Her medium brown eyes sparkled as the two of them discussed the countries represented on each light standard. She also appeared to be physically fit and stood about five foot six in her red sneakers. As she turned her tanned face to look at the man next to her, he put his hand in hers and kissed her lips with a tenderness that years of being two people who had become one embodied. There was a serenity to them that made me feel at peace. As they began to walk towards us I could hear the man ask the woman, "So…what time are the kids and the baby coming over for dinner?" "Seven," she answered. "Great! I can't wait," he responded. "Me too," she said. Then he looked at her and said, "I love you, honey." "I love you too," she responded as she brought his hand to her lips and kissed it, oblivious to the eyes that were watching them. They walked down to the pavement and up the Parkway towards 22nd Street.

Ed broke the silence. "See…love. It's an incredible thing. Doesn't it make you feel energized and at the same time tranquil. It's almost oxymoronic. But that kind of proves my point. Existence on different levels is there for us to enjoy. By opening our senses we were capable of experiencing a beautiful event; the interplay between that man and woman.

"As we stopped our conversation and opened our senses we became aware of other situations around us. If we do that on a consistent basis it's amazing how many sights, sounds, smells, feelings, and tastes we can deeply and richly enjoy.

"When you speak to guide someone, be cognizant that you don't display self-importance. Be aware of the difference between self-confidence and high self-esteem, which help us get along in the material world and may draw others towards us, and us towards them…and a big ego which can easily turn into selfishness and cause destruction of one's self and others.

"And when you've made your point or given the person or persons you're speaking with some guidance, stop speaking and let others process the information or give you their guidance. Remember, that whatever you may want to say you already know, be selective as to what you impart. We all know people who talk to hear themselves speak and speak over those already talking, and we know how it makes us feel. There are far too many preachers and not nearly enough guides."

"Geez," Ed continued. "I feel like I went on way too long and became preachy myself. Hmm…guess that's what might happen when you've held something inside for so many years and finally get into the company of old and trusted friends and let it out!"

"Preachy?" I added. "I don't think so Ed. Thought provoking yes, preachy, not at all." "If that was preachy, then you've given it a new definition Ed," Gail added.

"Thanks, of course I will take into consideration that those comments came from the two of you," Ed replied, still unsure of how the past few minutes were relayed.

"Believe me, we wouldn't placate you Ed," Gail admonished. "Ok, point made," Ed said with a nod.

Parting with an Old Pal

It was now late in the afternoon. Two months ago at this time it would have been dusk. The first rustlings of rush hour were upon us and the 'No parking after 4:30 p.m.' signs that were visible up and down the Parkway informed us that it was time for Gail to move her car.

I was the first to get up from our comfortable soft green 'conference room,' after looking at my watch and letting Gail and Ed know that we were five minutes from a parking ticket. The two of them bounced up, brushed themselves off and silently joined me as we walked towards the car.

Our little trek enabled me to think about what we had discussed and listen more intently to the passing cars, people and dogs as they moved up and down the thoroughfare. The birds sounded clearer, the trees, flowers and plants looked especially colorful and those beautiful flags sparkled brilliantly. It was as if a door in my mind, that had been previously unknown, had been found and opened. Everything looked, sounded, felt and smelled rich and panoramic. It was fantastic.

As we reached Gail's Toyota she told us that she would drop us off anywhere we'd like, but that she would have to go home and get ready for her Brother Jeffrey's birthday dinner at his house. We were distraught at knowing that Gail would be departing. It was as if the Three Musketeers were united again. What a shame to see our brief time together end.

We asked Gail if she would drop us off at Rittenhouse Square, the park where our day began.

"Before we pull away, let's exchange phone numbers, addresses and e-mail addresses, ok?" Gail asked.

"Great idea! Boy it would have been a bummer if you would have left us off at The Square and we didn't have each other's numbers," Ed replied.

Gail took a pen and some paper out of her glove compartment and we all wrote our information down and exchanged the sheets. She then started the car and pulled out of the parking space and made a right at 22nd Street, another right at the next street then went straight to 19th Street where she made yet another right turn and started to head for Rittenhouse Square.

"I'm missing you guys already," she said with watery eyes. "I hope I get to see you before I leave for Iceland in June."

"I have a feeling you'll see us more then once before you leave," I assured her.

"Remember what we talked about Gail," Ed interjected. "I hope you'll experience *Viewenic* situations and be able to teach us some important lessons when we hook-up again. 'Rise above it' Gail and bring back your knowledge. Look at yourself and life from up high, practice *Viewenics*. We'll be waiting to hear."

"You know I will," she responded with a lilt in her voice. "I've learned so much today and I'm so glad that you both decided to share things with me. Ed, I know that you and Chaz were supposed to spend the day together and I'm sure that you were planning to relate some things to him that you've been keeping inside for years. I'm honored that you also shared so much of it with me. I love you both and can't wait for the three of us to get back together again."

We were quickly approaching our destination. There, in front of us, was the park. Rush hour was in full bloom. We were stopped at the red light at 19th and Walnut Streets. Sadly, it was now time to leave Gail. If we waited for the signal to turn green to get out of the car we'd hear an enormous amount of horns blaring as we blocked the flow. Ed leaned over and kissed her on the cheek. I did the same from the back seat. We each grasped her right hand in succession, said that we loved her and would see her soon and then exited the car just as the light turned green.

As she made her right turn up Walnut Street she yelled out, "I love you both and let's get together real soon, you call me or I'll call you!" With that she waved and kept waving.

Ed and I stood on the corner waving as well, until her car was enmeshed in the myriad of other vehicles on their way out of Center City and out of sight.

"Wasn't it great to see Gail again?" I said rhetorically to Ed.

"Fantastic, simply fantastic…what a superb person she is Chaz. I'm looking forward to all of us getting together again without time constraints."

Entering the Square

We walked across Walnut Street and stood at the entrance to the park.

"So, my friend, we are where we started. Try not to let dogs take liberty with your shoes this time will ya!" Ed reminded me.

I laughed and gave him a smirk along with a sarcastic "Yeah, right!" just as two bicyclists zoomed behind us. They came so close that I turned to make sure that the back of my jeans was still attached to the front.

"Whew…whatever happened to bicycle horns or bells?" I asked Ed.

"Well…lemme think, don't know where the horns went but the bells were all secured by those ice-cream carts down the shore."

"Hey thanks! I never thought off that. But if anybody ever asked me, now I have the answer. Oh Great One…next can you tell me the mystery as to why Winky Dink went off television?"

"Winky Dink?" Whoa…Chaz you pulled one out of the time warp. "I'll find out and get back to ya."

We walked back into the park. As soon as we entered we spotted the perfect place to sit and continue our conversation. It was about ten yards past the entrance and twenty yards to the right, strategically situated in the shade of a huge tree.

Ed and I sat cross-legged as we looked at the inhabitants of the Square. The menagerie was consistent with my earlier observations except more and more people were showing up casually attired. Now that the workday had ended, the suits were replaced with sweats, tee shirts and jeans.

The two of us spent the first fifteen or so minutes just looking at, and listening to, our surroundings. For the first time I consciously worked at separating my self from myself. I observed my feet, legs, body and hands. Visualized my neck, face and head and started to view my body as if I was another entity. I felt myself rise up. It was not as difficult as I had imagined.

I could actually feel my perception of myself move further from my physical being. It was easy to view my feet, legs and hands as if they belonged to someone else…a someone else who was still me. The sounds of everything around me were prominent, while at the same time removed. I felt light and so did the air. I could feel my self rising above my being and it was incredible. It immediately occurred to me that if I continued to do these types of exercises I would be able to learn and enjoy the many facets of *Viewenics.* During this first *Viewenic* experience I was also concurrently cognizant of how fantastic it was.

Ed looked at me and asked, "You're having one, aren't you?"

"I was…thank you," I answered as I was removed from my newly realized state.

We laughed.

"Amazing isn't it?" he asked again.

"Yep, totally," I said – wishing I was still in it.

"You'll be able to get back at will, once you practice and get the hang of it."

"I know Ed. I entered it at will. I concentrated as you suggested earlier today and used some of the techniques you told me. What a phenomenal experience, I'm looking forward to studying and learning as much as I can."

"I'll be happy to work with you Chaz, as long as you work with me and help me."

"Help you? Help you with what?"

"Help me learn what you learn. Remember what I said earlier, never forget that the teacher becomes the student and the student becomes the teacher. It's a circle on a continuum. It's one of the basics of growth in everyone's ability to fully experience *Viewenics.*" Ed explained as he proceeded, "Over the past year I spent some time traveling and speaking with people about life and their lives in particular. I went to the Midwest, the South and the Caribbean, the West Coast and Canada. I took a short trip to Europe and one to Africa and spent a week in South America. It sounds like quite a bit, but believe me I spent a lot more time at home then I did on the road. Through it all, one thing I learned was that there's a hunger for a greater understanding of life from the inside out. People want to experience things first hand. They're tired of being told that these are the doctrines for this and the dogmas for that – that someone else sets the rules without their input. And beyond that lays the most predominant issue I came away with after thousands of conversations and thousands of miles, it's the fact that people know there's more to life than they've been led to believe.

"Chaz…people realize there's more but they haven't been able to manifest the vehicle to grasp it, learn from it and experience it. So, that's what the last year has given me, the understanding that everything I went through; from my parents cousins' club parties, to Ruth, Sam, Joan, the experience with my dad's passing and all the other *Viewenic* related occurrences, were events that ultimately led to the conclusion that it's time to help other people learn and teach and teach and learn, and grow."

"It's clear Ed, but how are you gonna start?"

"I already have. Today was the start. You were the beginning and Gail appropriately joined in. Amazing how that happened wasn't it?"

"Yes, I must say that it was pretty incredible. Not seeing her for all that time and then the two of us run into her together. I guess it was supposed to happen that way, eh?" I said as I shook my head.

I was officially hungry. Green tea and a smoothie don't make for much of a full stomach. I asked Ed if he was ready to chow down some food and he responded in the affirmative.

Dinner for Two

We lifted ourselves from the ground and looked across the park to 18th Street where three well-known restaurants were located. We strolled through the square and quickly saw the chairs of each eatery's outdoor café being occupied by the 'see and be seen' crowd of Center City.

As we walked leisurely along the concrete paths within the park we discussed our hungers and decided to eat at the seafood restaurant directly in front of us. The smell of freshly mowed grass was soon intermingled with the odor of bus fumes and the sounds of mass transit, cars and people yelling to each other over the din. We had arrived at the sidewalk and crossed 18th Street.

Deciding to eat inside, we strolled into Devon, the seafood restaurant, and were greeted by the host who inquired if it would just be the two of us. I told her it would, whereupon she led us down a few steps to a booth. The restaurant has the look of an old steakhouse, lots of wood and dark tables, chairs and booths. The bar, which we passed on the way to our table, seems to always be filled with young to middle-aged professionals looking to meet other young and middle-aged professionals. Kind of like the Match Game with alcohol. When I lived a few blocks away, a number of years ago, Devon was a Houlihan's and my girlfriend and I would come here on Wednesday nights to eat, drink, talk and watch the people who walked along the street and in the square.

Ed and I took our seats in the booth, which was next to an aisle that had a full view of the remainder of the dining room from where Ed sat and a clear sight line of the bar, entrance way and the rest of the front of the restaurant from my vantage point. We both had a partial view of the kitchen. The host gave each of us a large menu and told us that Cheryl would be our server. Shortly after we sat down, a young man filled our glasses with water and, a few moments later, brought us the restaurant's well-known biscuits. We left the prized delights and headed for the men's room to wash up before partaking of the fruits at hand. We settled in upon our return and stared at the soft golden brown sweet treats. No two are shaped exactly the same, although they all have the appearance of large blonde Easter Eggs with amber highlights on their roughly textured surfaces.

"Mmm…I love these," I said to Ed. "I could eat about twenty of 'em and forget the menu! Lemme make a biscuits sandwich" I went on as I cut mine in half, grabbed Ed's biscuit and put it between my two slices.

"Gimme that!" he said in mock anger. I gingerly handed it to him and, as he went to take it from me, I pulled my hand and his biscuit away. This went on two or three more times before he picked up his fork as if it was a weapon and reminded me that he was ready to duel for the succulent dough. We both laughed. Just then the young man who had given us the biscuits initially, walked by and, in an almost sleight of hand motion, grabbed another one from the basket he was carrying in his left hand with the tongs in his right and dropped it onto Ed's bread plate!

"Biscuit karma…nothin' like it," Ed said with an "I gotcha" sound to his voice.

I laid his first biscuit on top of his newly acquired gem and told him, "I ain't messin' with anybody who's got that much biscuit karma."

We opened our menu and within a few minutes both decided on the same meal – broiled salmon and a small salad.

Cheryl arrived; she was a pretty woman who appeared to be in her early twenties. She had short brown hair, pale skin and green eyes that smiled. She greeted us with a pleasant hello, introduced herself and asked us if we had decided on what we'd like to have for dinner.

We both told her we'd have the broiled salmon and a small green salad.

"Ok…and something to drink? She asked.

"Nah, nothin'…water's fine," I replied as she looked at Ed who shook his head in agreement.

As I so frequently do with servers, I asked Cheryl where she went to school.

Of course, if she wasn't attending school she would have said, "I don't." But most of the time the servers are students.

"Temple University," She answered.

"Hmm…and what are you majoring in?" I asked.

"Criminal justice," Cheryl said proudly.

"What made you decide to major in that?" I responded.

"Biscuit related murders," she said as she turned and laughed.

Ed and I both howled!

"That was funny; very, very, funny. We must have looked pretty pathetic to the rest of the restaurant mon ami, no?" Ed said still laughing hysterically.

"She gets a big tip, for the comedy alone," I added.

We wiped the tears from our eyes as Cheryl returned with our salads.

"You made our evening Cheryl…that was great!" Ed told her.

"My pleasure! You guys seemed to be having such a trauma over the biscuits I couldn't resist. Just kidding, it's actually fun to see people laughing and playing instead of being so serious. So many people who come in here seem to be ensconced in their business deals and problems, or intent on picking somebody up, that it's refreshing to watch people who are actually enjoying themselves. Don't get me wrong, it's not that it doesn't happen, it happens plenty…but still – just not enough for me. So…enjoy your salads and don't kill each other over the croutons."

Cheryl walked away as we all laughed at her last comment.

"She gets it," I said.

"Yes she does. I hope the criminal justice system appreciates her," Ed added.

We chomped away at our salads and biscuits as if we hadn't eaten in months. Our bread plates received their refills, which we quickly consumed, while our salads disappeared in record time.

Cheryl returned with our entrees "Salmon, vegetables, rice avec citron for the two vacuum cleaners," she said as she put the plates down in front of each of us.

"Merci…merci beaucoup," Ed replied as he reminded her to make sure that 'Mr. Hoover' over there – pointing in my direction – gets another biscuit.

"Oui," she said as she stood at attention, saluted, turned, and walked towards the kitchen.

"Geez…she even ends things in French!" Ed chuckled delightedly.

"Fantastic," I added.

"She picked up our energy immediately," Ed observed. "And she seemed to flow effortlessly into our conversation and life. She is indeed a pleasure to be around. I wonder what her goals are. It would be interesting to know."

Amanda Appears

The salmon looked moist and delicious. The first bite reinforced my observation. The texture filled my palate with a perfect softness, not so soft as to lose its consistency yet soft enough to be easily enjoyed. As we both savored our main course. We were interrupted by a young voice. Mr. Elias? Mr. Samuel?

"Yes," we responded in unison.

"It's Amanda Steinberg, Bob's daughter."

"Amanda?" Ed said with a bit of disbelief in his voice. "Look at you! The last time we saw you was at your sweet sixteen party! I know this sounds trite, but you're all grown up...geez it's unbelievable! How are you? And how are your dad, mom and brother?"

"Everybody's doing great. Mom still has the advertising firm and dad's medical practice is as busy as ever, seems like everybody wants cosmetic surgery. Larry just graduated Penn, he's going on to med school in the fall and I've been at Billar, Morton, and Black for three years now doing corporate law."

"Huh!?" I said in disbelief at the time warp I felt was in my midst.

"Yep...three years, amazing isn't it?" she said, swelling with pride.

"I can't believe I saw both of you. I'm waiting for a couple of my coworkers and I was looking around to see if they were here when I saw a server salute these two men she was waiting on, and lo and behold, they were you."

"Here Amanda, sit down," I said, as I motioned her to sit next to me. "You'll be able to see everyone who walks in, this way you can update us some more and not miss your colleagues when they come in."

"Thanks, I will. How are you guys?"

"We're well. We're spending the day together after not seeing each other for over a year," Ed told her.

"Gee, that's a long time for you two not to see each other," Amanda remarked – knowing full well how close Ed and I have been over the years.

I was at the hospital only a few hours after she was born. Bob called me to tell me the news of her birth and I drove to the hospital as quickly as I could. Obviously, that was the first time I saw her. I watched her grow over the years. The last time I saw her, Amanda was a young woman of sixteen. She was always smart and savvy beyond her years. It doesn't surprise me that she's a lawyer. We would kid her when she'd discuss politics, the economy, and social issues with any of us. We'd tell her that she sounded like a lawyer in front of a jury, pleading her case to anyone who'd listen.

Both Ed and I were close with her dad when we were in college. Bob met Sarah, her mom, at a Moody Blues concert. It was love at first sight. They became inseparable. We all hung out together and when I got married and Ed followed suit, the six of us got together every weekend. Then, as time passed, we saw less and less of Bob and Sarah, not because we didn't want to but because of business travels, family issues, and then divorce and other obligations. The last time Ed and I saw Bob and Sarah was also at Amanda's sweet sixteen affair.

Now here was Amanda, looking just like the lawyer we always thought she'd be, in her crisp charcoal gray pinstriped jacket and skirt, white blouse and black pumps. Her hair was straight to her shoulders and black, the same color as her eyes. Attractive and professional is how she would best be described with an overriding air of kindness and caring.

Cheryl returned to check on us and deliver another serving of biscuits. However, this time they were accessorized…in each sweet mound was a fork, stuck straight down into its center, prongs piercing its innards like a pitchfork in a bale of hay. It reminded me of the mythical sword that

King Arthur had so heroically withdrawn from the stone that Merlin had fused it into.

"Biscuit dueling at six o'clock...gentlemen your swords!" she stated. She then nodded at Amanda and said "My Lady" and with a bow and a wink she was off, only to return a few seconds later with the dessert tray.

"So gang, dessert?" Cheryl asked. Ed, Amanda and I looked at each other.

"None for me, I'm gonna have dinner in a couple of minutes," Amanda announced as she shook her head no. Ed and I, on the other hand, were enthralled by what looked like ten superb choices that Cheryl so elegantly balanced on a large brown tray.

"Whatcha got there?" I asked. Cheryl lowered the tray onto the edge of the table to enable us to see the items as she ran through the descriptions of the each delectable treat. I ordered the crème brulee and Ed requested the double chocolate layer cake, forgoing such temping things as: key lime pie, strawberry mouse cheese cake, and one of my all-time favorites...the coconut sorbet with caramel sauce.

Cheryl was off like a jet after a quick "gotcha...I'll be right back."

Amanda chuckled and stated, "She's somethin', isn't she!?"

"Yep," we both added in unison.

Amanda perused the crowd in and around the bar and entranceway wondering if perhaps her buddies had arrived without her knowledge. The place was teeming with people. It was now a few minutes before six. The office buildings had released their inhabitants en masse, and it seemed like a sizable portion of them, along with a large number of Center City residents, decided to head directly for Devon. However none of new arrivals were Amanda's coworkers.

Goals and Desires

I was curious to know about Amanda's goals and desires and proceeded to ask her if she had any specific objectives in her life.

Her answers seemed typical of a young lawyer on the fast track. "I want to be a partner in the firm, be recognized as an expert in my area, be respected by my colleagues and clients, own a nice house in center city, earn a substantial income and have all the comforts that come with my position."

"Interesting," was my response and Ed nodded in agreement.

Amanda spoke proudly of her objectives as if to intimate that she would be a raging success in her field.

Deep inside I was puzzled. I was about to ask Amanda a follow-up question when Cheryl arrived with our desserts, which she placed gently in front of us.

My crème Brule was magnificent in its small white casserole dish, the sugar on its top was burnt to a soft golden brown, the sweet beige pudding below and a raspberry perched in its center screamed…eat me! Ed's double chocolate layer cake oozed dark chocolate from between its rich layers of floury succulent deep dark cake, which was imbedded with dark chocolate chips and topped with shaved dark chocolate. Mmm…

Ed picked up his fork and I grabbed my spoon. However, before we could take our first bite Cheryl had to ask us a question. "How are you guys gonna eat these things after devouring forty-two biscuits?"

"Thanks for the encouragement," I said. "We'll find a way."

"But before you tiptoe off to another table Ms. Detective, I've got a question for you."

Cheryl looked at me with a mock expression that emitted an, "Ok... what is it?" gesture.

"What are your goals in life?" I asked.

"Huh? You want an answer to that in 30 seconds?" she laughed "Alright...here goes. I want to graduate and get into the criminal justice system to work with investigators. I also want to work with crime victims to help them adjust their lives after their traumas while working to bring closure to their situations and bring the perpetrators to justice. I'd like to become so proficient at what I do that others look to me for guidance. But most of all I'd like to meet a nice guy who I'm in love with and he with me, get married, have kids and have a house full of love, respect, joy, and caring. Ultimately, isn't that what everyone wants? After all, life isn't just about business, your occupation or position is it?" she stated rhetorically.

The three of us, almost in unison said, "You're right."

And with that Cheryl bowed and took off for the next table.

Amanda looked at us with embarrassment. "I feel like my answer was so shallow compared to Cheryl's. You know guys, what she ultimately wants is what I really want too; love, a family, and a house full of joy. The rest of the stuff is just a game...a game I enjoy...but just a game. It's the love part that's real."

"That was my next question for you Amanda. I was getting ready to ask you what you REALLY wanted in life when Cheryl came over to the table. I guess she understands...and you do too! Ya know, it gives a new meaning to that old expression...'Love conquers all.'"

Amanda smiled as Ed winked and we proceeded to dig into our desserts.

"Why is it that we lose our perspectives so quickly?" Amanda asked.

"Because we allow ourselves to," was Ed's – muffled by a mouthful of chocolate cake – reply. "The game overruns the real; we redirect our energies into less relevant activities and rationalize them into relevance. We've also become very good at commoditizing everything. Our culture tends to put dollar values even on things that are priceless, like life itself."

"How do we regain real relevance?" Amanda asked as I motioned to her to try my now half consumed crème brulee.

She politely said no, reminding me once again that she would soon be having dinner.

"We regain relevance by looking at how we interact with our environment, by separating our selves from ourselves so that we can view things from a fuller, broader perspective, and by understanding how all energy is interconnected and what our part is in that connection," was Ed's answer.

"That's a very short explanation to a substantially more complicated answer, but I hope you get the gist," he continued.

Amanda pulled out a pad and a pen from her purse and said, "I want to write that down, would you repeat that Ed?"

As Ed stated his thoughts once more, Amanda jotted them down and mentioned that she would contemplate their meaning and hoped that she could call Ed to further the discussion. She asked us if we would be able to get together with her in the future or if we ever thought about having a regular discussion group to tackle these issues.

Ed said yes to each of her quarries and mentioned that he would love it if the three of us could meet again. He also said that if she would bring her dad, mom and brother along that would be great too.

An Arrival of Friends

Amanda was so engrossed in our discussion that she didn't notice the three young men and two young women in dark business suits pointing at her as they moved in our direction. They were obviously her coworkers. All five of them looked like they had just walked out of the pages of the latest fashion magazine for lawyers. Each of them was nattily attired. Shoes shined, the men's ties loosely knotted indicating that the day was long and that it was now time to relax, yet not so much so as to untie them completely.

They arrived at our table and Amanda began to introduce each one of them with a short resume, after a brief description of who we were. "Guys these are two of my dad's and my mom's oldest and dearest friends, they've known me since I was born. I'd like you to meet Ed Elias and Chaz Samuel." We graciously shook each person's hand. "And these are my close compadres and fellow legal eagles," as she began to single out her buddies. "This is Semi Ackuzi, he's originally from Zimbabwe, studied at Temple and now he's a Philly guy and a damn good corporate attorney. And...this is Jung Chen Yi, he came over from China about fifteen years ago, got his international law degree from Penn and now he's with our international group, and Sally Simmons here specializes in patent law, she's from Mount Airy like us! And, she's another Temple Owl."

They all seemed quite proud of their accomplishments as Amanda continued. "This is Bob Martin, I've known Bob since I was 10, in fact – he was at my Sweet Sixteen party too! Hmmm...maybe you talked to each other back then. Anyway, Bob is in tax law...a Villanova grad and was the top guy in his class at Central High!"

Amanda knew how much Central High meant to both Ed and I. We both graduated from, what was then, the number one academic high school in the country and is the second oldest high school in the country. It's still right up there with the best schools and has an alumni and Hall of Fame that's second to none.

"And finally, Amanda continued, this is my next door neighbor Kiesha Washington. Our offices are right next to each other and we've become dependent on each other's expertise. We're practically a team. We went to Temple Law together. When she was hired, they asked her which students she would recommend to join the firm. And...she recommended me! Kiesha's why I'm at Billar, Morton, and Black. She won so many honors in Law School that she was recruited by firms from all over the country... but once a Philly girl, always a Philly girl!"

"Well...what a pleasure it is to meet such a fine group of attorneys. If ever I need any legal help I sure know who to call now!" I said.

Ed added, "Listen gang, when you walk over to your table, please don't slip on anything or it'll be total confusion as to who's gonna represent whom in the personal injury suit!"

After a few minutes of laughter and banter, Amanda got up and joined her friends. Everyone shook hands once again and we exchanged final pleasantries. Amanda made sure that the three of us exchanged phone numbers and reminded us that she'd be in touch. We sent our regards to her family and off went the Billar, Morton, and Black legal team.

"Lemme see," Ed pondered, "that's about eighty billion dollars in educational costs," he chuckled, knowing how exaggerated his statement was. "And, they still ultimately want the same things that a Yanamamo Indian in the rain forest, an Australian Aborigine, a retail sales clerk, a police officer, or a judge wants. A game...Amanda hit it squarely on the head...a game."

Leaving Devon

Within a few minutes Ed and I had finished our deserts. The last tiny piece of cake was hanging from the corner of Ed's mouth like a lonely Christmas ornament on the side of the tree that faces the corner. I brushed my hand across my mouth as I looked at Ed and said, "Ahem." He caught my drift and wiped the morsel off his face with his finger, then put the last remnant in his mouth as he launched into a low, long, mmm… followed by a satiated, "That was great."

Cheryl stopped by and asked if there was anything else we needed.

"No," I said. "You've given us all the food we required plus quite a bit of wisdom that we desired. Cheryl, you're a delight. We'll ask for you the next time we come in."

She politely thanked us and told Ed and I how much fun she had waiting on the 'dynamic duo.' She put the check on the table as she moved to the station next to us after the two people in the booth motioned for her attention.

Ed and I split the check and added an extra twenty-five percent for the excellent service and laughs that Cheryl had bestowed on two old buddies who enjoyed every moment of her service.

As we exited the booth to make our way into the crowd and onto the sidewalk we handed the cash and check to Cheryl, each of us bowing in reverence to the wise young woman who helped make our eating experience so pleasant. She bowed back, smiled, thanked us again and requested our return.

We left Devon satisfied, both physically and mentally.

The End Starts The Beginning

The sky had become dark. Night on 'The Square' was a beautiful sight. The trees glistened with tiny yellow lights that gave them a holiday appearance all year round. People swarmed into all the restaurants and it seemed like hundreds were now occupying their sidewalk café tables. The mood was jovial. Laughing, eating, toasting, and talking above the din of the automobiles, as they slowly made their way along 18th street, were the common themes.

As we crossed the street to get back to where we began our daylong journey, I started to view the entire scene from above. The park was magnificent, the festivities energizing, the city beautiful. I looked down upon them while I stepped onto the pavement. I was doing it instantly now while, at the same time, fully aware of my on-ground presence and connections. Fantastic.

Ed turned to me as we approached the bench where we had laughed so heartily about the streaming pooch. "My friend, we have just begun – I know you understand the method now, I noticed it as we ventured into the park. You are solidly with me on this trip. It's time for me to go. I have some things to work on and places to see. But I will be back here tomorrow evening if you have the time."

He was fully aware that I had put the next night, and more, on my schedule for him. I wouldn't miss his presence for anything. I was thrilled to be with him. My mind was brimming with thoughts of what was to come. I couldn't wait for tomorrow, yet I was quite content with now. The feelings of serenity and excitement were concurrently occupying my brain. I will be viewing my world tonight as never before.

"You know I'll be here Ed…we still have to go over the Phillies stats and we haven't discussed why people make Jell-0 molds of past Vice-Presidents and Secretaries of States."

Ed laughed; we hugged and vowed to call each other during the day to set up the exact time. We already knew the place.

He walked away towards the direction from whence he came earlier in the day. His being seemed to glow through the darkness of the square. As he reached the exit on the far side he raised his right arm and waved his hand, indicating "so long" for now. He never turned around to see if I was looking but I was certain that he knew I was.

Today I gained a new and wiser perspective on life. Tonight I look forward to the treat of never before experienced travels, and tomorrow… more wisdom.

A Summary of Soaring

The Lessons of Soaring:

Separate your self from yourself
Rise above it
Laugh
Keep life in perspective
Love is what really matters
Everyone needs love, respect, joy and caring
Business is a game
Recognize when you've been commoditized

Quotes from and for Soaring

"You know Chaz, people are amazing. We have so much power within our minds, bodies and souls but so few of us take advantage of it."

"Remember this Chaz...life should be fun and there should also be lots of funny in life. I once read somewhere that, *'Laughing at ourselves is the tonic that keeps us sane.'* That's one of my favorite sayings...it really sums up an important aspect of life quite well. People spend so much of their lives thinking about the past while not focusing on the all-important present and their plans for the immediate, mid-range and distant future. There are so many neat things out there just waiting to be experienced! Plus, too many people take life way too seriously and harbor those energy zapping emotions; regret, guilt, jealousy and worry, not to mention greed and hate. And they actually think that material things, business success and position are more important than loving others and themselves, laughing and hugging and enjoying the fruits of nature. It's sad, very sad. And it's perpetuated by our society. It takes a strong person to see through it. That doesn't mean that you can't enjoy the finer things in life. What has happened however is that so many people have allowed those things to control them, instead of the other way around."

"Energy flows, it doesn't really disappear. Some of the energy may be in different forms or places, but it's still with us, the same energy that Washington used to keep his men motivated at Valley Forge, the same energy that Franklin used to run his printing presses, the same energy that people used to build the underground railroad, to help free the slaves in the mid 1800s, under some of the structures we're passing right now. It doesn't go away, it just doesn't," Ed relayed with certainty.

"Focusing your energy is like using a laser. It can take you to places you never thought you would reach. It's all about transcending your physical self," Ed stated as we rounded the corner.

"Then, suddenly, there I was, downstairs watching everyone enjoying themselves, telling jokes, talking, drinking and eating, shaking hands and holding hands, laughing and relaxing. However, I wasn't exactly there. I was floating above them all, maybe three feet that's all, and I had the ability to witness the entire scene. I soon realized no one could see me. Yet, I could see myself. I could look down and see my body, arms and legs as I floated along. I was like an invisible bird. I loved it. I was king of my little world, the great observer. And no one, not even my mom or dad, could see me. It was amazing."

"Thanks. So if your radio can pick up signals or energy waves and your television can pick up energy waves and the radio and TV towers can send out those waves, what do you think your mind does or can do?"

"As we looked at each other to begin our conversation a strange thing happened. All of a sudden a bright white beam of light with a slight blue tint appeared, emanating from the middle of my forehead to the middle of Victor's. It was in the same location that the mystics refer to as the third eye. There was no need to talk because all the information that Victor and I wanted to exchange was flowing into our minds along that beam of light. It was absolutely incredible. No sound, no voice, just pure thought."

"It amuses me when I read certain self-help authors who state rather unequivocally that humans have higher intelligence than animals and possess attributes like free will and other skills that separate us from other species. I always want to call them up and ask them, 'How the heck do you know that?' It amazes me that some people can be so ethnocentric, or species centric, that they believe that other species can't possibly posses the same, different, greater, or more intuitive, faculties than we do as a species."

"I'm very serious. Energy's an awesome thing. It can move earth, bring us light, grow our food, enable us to walk and talk…why shouldn't it visit us in other forms? It goes back to what you said about '*astonishing being an understatement.*' For some reason I couldn't argue with that."

"It was about concentrating your energy and being open to receive incoming energy as well. Do you think that the only things that can receive sound, radio, television or any other kind of waves are just the instruments that were built to receive them? Or do you think that it's possible for some other vehicle to intercept those waves or pick up those waves in addition to the item that was built for that purpose? Ponder this, if a million radios can pick up the same signal why can't someone's mind act as a receiver as well and be number one million and one?"

"After doing all that research and still not coming up with a totally viable explanation, I began to realize that perhaps the reason I couldn't find a word to describe my experiences was because no one had categorized it in a manner that would enable it to have one. So I set about thinking of a word that would capture the separation of the spiritual self from the physical self while still being connected to each other."

"I decided to call it *Viewenics,*" Ed went on, "a combination of the ability to view one's surroundings from a broader perspective, while understanding that it incorporates energy and is based in the principles of physics."

"The phrase, 'out of body experience,' just didn't capture the full essence of the knowledge I had gained. As the days passed, I noticed that I could, in fact, remove my 'self' from my body at will. I could stand back and look at myself, and how I interacted with my environment. It gave me an energy flow that was free and open.

"You see, one thing that we as humans have become very good at is filtering everything through our values and beliefs systems, even what happens to us and our energy. And that creates judgmental reactions and a hazy view of what actually is. I tried to explain that to Sam."

"Because, once we start taking ourselves too seriously…it's over"

"I really felt that when I saw myself on top of that mountain I wasn't anyone special. I just felt as if I was someone who had realized a gift that we all have, including the people below. I will say however…that the view was spectacular, as all my *Viewenic* views are. And, that I also believed that I was looking at people who were from a land of leaders, people leading themselves while taking in and sending out love for and from everyone."

"If the teacher is a guide, someone who points them in a direction, rather than telling them that this is where they are, and need to be, the student can discover new vistas on his or her own. The teacher helps but doesn't control. That enables the student to have a map and make the discoveries on his or her own, which is far more enthralling and much easier to absorb. And, it also allows the student to teach the teacher new things."

"Once you separate your self from yourself and gain the *Viewenic* ability to see things from afar, you begin to understand how everything is related to everything else. You notice how hurting someone or something else means that you're ultimately hurting yourself. You can see and feel how all energy, and therefore everything, is interconnected. What purpose does it serve to take and not give, accept and not learn, teach and not understand, stifle your mind and not grow? These points, as timeless as some of them seem, are still not fully understood and experienced."

"It's our responsibility to learn, grow, understand, and pass on the knowledge so that others will do the same. You know that it's a circle. We lead by following and follow by leading. That's why everyone is involved. We're all equal and we all have the same abilities, none greater and none lesser. The energy is continuous. It's wonderful to know it and see it and pass it on and have others pass it on and back again to the original guide who then experiences something new for himself or herself."

"When you've mastered *Viewenics* you've given real meaning to the term 'rise above it.' Isn't it amazing that that term is so often used without people really thinking about its meaning? It's the perfect *Viewenic* expression. Rise above it, literally, and you will understand that you are constantly meditating. With *Viewenics* you are living a yogic existence. It enables you to live horizontally and vertically at the same time. You can go through life on infinite planes, because you're tapping into the universal energy that's already there, just waiting to be experienced. All most people need in order to encounter it is a guide. And once they've achieved it they can become a guide for someone else, and the understanding and experiencing of *Viewenics* will grow with guides teaching and learning everywhere, so that everyone can become a spiritual guide. That would create an environment of inclusiveness and equality on a spiritual level not seen on this earth for a very long time, if ever. Everyone would be a leader! Imagine the energy!"

"As we stopped our conversation and opened our senses we became aware of other situations around us. If we do that on a consistent basis it's amazing how many sights, sounds, smells, feelings, and tastes we can deeply and richly enjoy."

"When you speak to guide someone, be cognizant that you don't display self-importance. Be aware of the difference between self-confidence and high self-esteem, which help us get along in the material world and may draw others towards us, and us towards them…and a big ego which can easily turn into selfishness and cause destruction of one's self and others."

"And when you've made your point or given the person or persons you're speaking with some guidance, stop speaking and let others process the information or give you their guidance. Remember, that whatever you may want to say you already know, be selective as to what you impart. We all know people who talk to hear themselves speak and speak over those already talking, and we know how it makes us feel. There are far too many preachers and not nearly enough guides."

"Help me learn what you learn. Remember what I said earlier, never forget that the teacher becomes the student and the student becomes the teacher. It's a circle on a continuum. It's one of the basics of growth in everyone's ability to fully experience *Viewenics*."

"The game overruns the real; we redirect our energies into less relevant activities and rationalize them into relevance. We've also become very good at commoditizing everything. Our culture tends to put dollar values even on things that are priceless, like life itself."

"We regain relevance by looking at how we interact with our environment, by separating our selves from ourselves so that we can view things from a fuller, broader perspective, and by understanding how all energy is interconnected and what our part is in that connection."

About The Author

Dan Goldberg is a nationally recognized keynote speaker, author, coach, trainer, and entrepreneur.

He was the founder and former owner of the highly successful multi-national optical company 'For Eyes,' whose cutting edge approach to the sale of eyewear and related services irrevocably changed the entire industry and had a major impact on how all service businesses are marketed. Subsequently, he created an international management, marketing, public relations and advertising firm; putting his prowess to work for clients in both the for-profit and non-profit sectors.

He has been the subject of stories in *Newsweek, Business Week, Playboy, Successful Business, Investor's Business Daily*, as well as major newspapers in New York, Philadelphia, Washington, D.C., Boston, Baltimore, Miami, San Francisco, Oakland, St. Louis, Chicago, Los Angeles and many other national and local publications. In addition, Dan has appeared on *Good Morning America* and other national and local television and radio programs.

His frequent keynote speeches, lectures and training sessions are filled with insights about life, contentment, success, and leadership; and are always peppered with lots of laughter. His sense of humor and comedic flair were honed from his time as a stand-up comic and writer while working with some of today's best known comedians and entertainers.

He is the author of the books *"Lighten Up and Lead"* and "*Stand Back A Second, Just Don't Fall Off The Edge,"* co-author, with Don Martin, of the book, *"The Entrepreneur's Guide To Successful Leadership"* and author of "*The Six Steps To Solid Sales Success™*" and "*The Seven Elements Of Successful Leadership™*" programs. He is an adjunct professor at the Fox School of Business, Temple University, the Smeal College of Business, Penn State University, and Kutztown University's College of Business. He received his Bachelor of Arts degree from Temple University and his Master of Business Administration degree from Kutztown University.

websites:
www.dangoldberg.net – www.soaringlife.com – www.dangoldberg.com